Rescued Recipes

From My Grandmother's Trash Can

To Jan Marie,

Happy Cooking!

Enjoy!

Lisa Canino

Lisa Canino

Rescued Recipes
Copyright © 2015 Lisa Canino
ISBN 978-1-63381-037-2
Library of Congress Control Number: 2015902735

Designed and produced by
Maine Authors Publishing
558 Main Street
Rockland, Maine 04841
www.maineauthorspublishing.com

Printed in the United States of America

For my family

Introduction

It all started with a birthday—my mother's, to be precise, and I had spent countless hours fretting about presents and cake.

Every year, prior to her birthday, Mother's Day, and Christmas, Ma always said, "You know what I'd really like is…." What she always wanted was for me to give some of my time throughout the year without any sighs or excuses. I rarely fulfilled these requests. Before this particular birthday, she asked for the usual, but also wanted the photograph of my youngest daughter that she had been bugging me for, some personalized address labels, a bio on Pat Conroy, and the deed to a family cemetery plot. Given that it was the celebration of her 80th year of life on this planet, who could say no?

While searching through family memorabilia for the cemetery deed, I came across a manila folder. In it were some handwritten recipes. As I thought back, I remembered my mother telling me that she had rescued these from a trash can in my Grandmother Austin's house. Since I am the family historian and "keeper of the keys," my mother gave the recipes to me.

Several years earlier, Gram had slowly started to slip into the topsy-turvy world of dementia, and had developed the habit of discarding important documents—including bills—into the kitchen trash can. So on her weekly visits to Gram's house, Ma would empty the trash can, bring the contents home with her, and set aside items of significance. You might ask why she didn't just rummage through the rubbish while she was at Gram's house. Well, first of all, Gram had developed a cantankerous disposition, and would have questioned the need for my mother to dig through her garbage; and second, I'm pretty sure Ma was trying to preserve what was left of Gram's gradually fading sense of dignity.

Getting sidetracked in my mission to discover where deceased relatives were buried, I started leafing through the manila folder of worn and soiled pages, wondering why Gram had chosen to throw out these recipes.

Prior to their discovery in that trash can, my mother had never seen these recipes before, and Gram had never made any of them for her or for me, even though they *certainly* contained some of her favorite foods. Questions arose.

The recipes appeared to be old, but *how* old were they? When and from whom did Gram acquire them? Names I did not know flashed out at me from the depths of the folder. Who were Edith Leonard, Jenny Ray, and Mrs. White? Were they neighbors or friends? I knew that Mother Earle was Gram's first mother-in-law—her full name was Lizzie Earle—and she was a very special grandmother who provided my mother with happy childhood memories, just like Gram did for me. Was she the author of these pages? If so, are the stains that adorn these papers just soil from a trash bin, or evidence of a dutiful daughter-in-law's culinary attempts as a young wife? Were these recipes some of my grandfather's favored victuals, too?

Gram married Edward "Ted" Earle in 1929, and after a decade of turbulence, she walked out of the marriage one day. So why did she hang onto the recipes all these years? With no one to fill in the blanks and Gram having gone to meet her maker, it was clear that these questions would remain a mystery until we met again.

Casting aside uncertainties, I resumed perusing the folder, and one of the timeworn recipes stood out among the others: Mother Earle's Sour Milk Spice Cake. I thought, wouldn't it be great to surprise Ma with this? I had been scouring my cookbook collection for days trying to find the perfect birthday cake recipe, and I finally found it here among these rescued pages. I pulled the recipe out and set the folder aside until I had time for further exploration.

So on the eve of the big day, I donned my thinking cap, and set out to decipher and create a masterpiece out of a recipe with very few directions—not even the kind of pan to use, oven temperature, or cooking time.

With what seemed to be the right mixture of spice, sweetness, and texture, the cake went into the oven. With prayers said, I stared through the oven door window, watching the batter rise and turn a deliciously golden brown color. The smell was incredible! As I laid the pan on a rack to cool, it took every ounce of resistance I could muster not to sample a piece. I was so proud of myself!

The next day, I made a few accompaniments (homemade cinnamon applesauce and fresh whipped cream) to serve with the birthday cake. After creating an artistic copy of the recipe on my trusty computer, I packed up the goodies along with the "gifts," and left the dooryard, beaming as I set off for the birthday girl's house.

After lunch and a champagne toast, it was time to open the presents. I waited anxiously for Ma to open mine and find her grandmother's recipe.

When the moment finally arrived, she asked, "What's this?"

Instead of giving her a moment to figure it out on her own, I blurted out with excitement, "That's one of the recipes you pulled out of Gram's trash can. It's your Grandmother Earle's recipe, and that's the cake I made for you." Although her response was less than anticipated, the first forkful of cake eased my disappointment as we all exclaimed that Mother Earle's Sour Milk Spice Cake was delicious!

As we sat around digesting my epicurean delight, conversation centered on family, politics, and upcoming events. We talked about how I was near completing my lifelong dream of graduating from a culinary program, and my idea about writing a post-graduation cookbook. Our chat lead to the topic of those rescued recipes, and Ma exclaimed, "Hey, there is an idea for your cookbook. Use those." So I did, and this book is the result.

I knew that first I needed to take these recipes from bygone days, test them, and bring them into the 21st century. I scoured vintage cookbooks from the late 1800s to the 1930s in used bookstores and on library shelves, and referenced my own collection for clues that might help me produce an edible product from the limited information provided with each recipe.

Two years, zillions of calories, and countless trips to grocery stores later, I finished testing and devouring the last rescued recipe. Some were more challenging than others, and some I just gave up on. Tweaking was necessary for a few, to make them a little more flavorful, and I even created a few inspired versions of my own. Following advice from great cooks, I used the freshest and highest quality ingredients available to me. The final products gave me a newfound respect and love for old-fashioned food made with simple ingredients.

With every measurement and stir, Gram kept creeping into my mind. Even though she had never made any of these rescued recipes *for* me, she seemed to be making them *with* me, as recollections of happy times in her company and the food we shared danced in my head. So somehow, I wanted this to become more than just a cookbook. I wanted it to include snippets and stories about the woman behind these tattered and discarded pages of gastronomic wonders, and to share the ways in which she provided me with the inspiration to fulfill a dream.

Enjoy!

Mildred Arline (Knox, Earle) Austin
1908–2006

Meet Gram

Afeisty Mainer who had lived through the Great Depression, Gram lived to the ripe old age of 97. The oldest of seven children born to Harry D. and Millie Frances (Hartford) Knox, she grew up on a farm in Berwick, Maine that had been in her family for generations.

Throughout her life, she experienced many heartbreaks that never broke her stoic and resilient nature. At the age of 16, Gram found herself in charge of her younger siblings after her mother died suddenly on the day after Christmas in 1924. Years later, in 1943, her father died at the age of 57. Gram divorced her first husband when her three children were in their fledgling years and her second husband, the love of her life, Maurice "Sonny" Austin, died in 1963 at the age of 56. Sonny had just sold his gas station and retired. She lost her only son, Robert Earle, in 1998, and outlived all of her siblings.

Gram was a college graduate, and had a happy career as a secretary. During World War II, she was a member of the Drivers Corps, and was a certified First Aid Member of the Red Cross. In January 1960, she attended President John F. Kennedy's Inauguration after having procured two of Senator Margaret Chase Smith's twelve allotted tickets.

She was blessed with a grand laugh and a marvelous sense of humor. A cousin once summed up her personality perfectly: "She was a character who always had something going on."

Gram had twelve grandchildren and several great-grandchildren, and provided some unforgettable moments to treasure. Our lives would not have been the same without her.

Gram and my nephew Josh in the woods of Maine, July 1990

THE RESCUED RECIPES

Earle Gingerbread

½ cup sugar   ½ cup molasses
1 " flour   1 beaten egg
1 teaspoon melted butter
½ teaspoon soda
¼   "   nutmeg, cinnamon + all spice
        ½ cup boiling water
Mix well together. Add hot water
last. Bake in moderate oven.

Pineapple Cocoanut Pie

Heat 1½ cups milk. Mix 4 tablespoons
flour, ½ teaspoon salt, ½ cup sugar
add hot milk and cook in
double boiler about 20 minutes
or until mixture is thick and
flour thoroughly cooked. Pour
onto 2 egg yolks, return to double
boiler and cook until eggs thicken,
or about 3 minutes. Cool, add 1
cup well-drained pineapple, ½ cup
shredded cocoanut and ½ teaspoon
vanilla. Pour into baked pie crust
Cover with meringue, sprinkle with
cocoanut and brown.

Mother Earle's Sour Milk Spice Cake

1 egg, 1 cup sugar, 1/4 teaspoon cinnamon
                              ,,   ,,   clove
                              ,,   ,,   nutmeg
almost 1/2 cup melted shortening
1 cup sour milk, 1 teaspoon soda
stirred in milk. About 2 cups flour.
Raisins can be used + if so use a
little more flour.

"Chocolate Cake"

1/4 cup butter	1/2 cup water
1 cup sugar	1 1/2 cups flour
1 egg	1 1/2 teaspoons baking powder
1 teaspoon vanilla	1/2 teaspoon salt
	2 heaping tablespoons cocoa

Cream butter and sugar + unbeaten egg.
Mix and add vanilla and cocoa. Then
add part of the water + part of flour
and other dry sifted together.

"Frosting"

1 1/2 tablespoons butter
2 cups powdered sugar
1 1/2 teaspoons cocoa
4-5 tablespoons hot milk
     Cream the butter. Add sugar. Add
chocolate + milk.

"Chocolate Frosting"

3/4 cup sugar   2 squares chocolate
(3 tablespoons milk   1 egg yolk
Melt chocolate, add sugar and milk.
Cook in double boiler until smooth.
add egg yolk and cook 1 min. - spread
on cake.

"Butter Frosting"

2 tablespoons cream   Butter size of egg
Powdered sugar to make stiff   Flavoring
  Beat well. Cocoa may be used.

"Mocha Frosting"

1 cup powder sugar   2 teaspoons cocoa
1 teaspoon vanilla   Butter size of walnut
2 tablespoons boiling coffee
  Cream sugar, cocoa and butter, then
add the coffee, then the vanilla.

"Brown Sugar Frosting"

1 cup brown sugar   2 tablespoons boiling water
White of 1 egg
  Boil sugar and water 5½ min., after
it begins to bubble vigorously, beat
white of egg stiff. Pour syrup over egg
and beat until ready to spread. 1/3 t. vanilla.

"Delicious Chocolate Cake"
2 squares chocolate or ½ cup cocoa, ½ cup
sweet milk. Cook on stove stirring
steadily till thickened. Remove from
fire and stir in ⅓ cup butter, 1 cup sugar,
1 teaspoon Vanilla, another ½ cup milk
with 1 rounding teaspoon soda
dissolved in it. 1½ cups, measured before
sifting, beat well. Bake in moderate oven.

"Angel Gingerbread"

½ cup sugar   ¼ cup molasses
1 egg   ¼ " shortening (butter or lard)
¼ teaspoon cinnamon 1 heaping cup flour
1 teaspoon ginger
    Beat this well, then add ½ cup boiling
water in which dissolve 1 teaspoon
soda. Serve with whipped cream.

"Maple Syrup Cake"

1½ cups maple syrup, ½ cup granulated sugar,
Scant half cup shortening, 1 cup heavy sour
milk, 1 teaspoon soda, pinch of salt
Flavor with ginger or mixed spices (
(cinnamon, clove + nutmeg) Mix thin as for
any soft ginger bread, 2 eggs well beaten
and stir in lightly the last thing.

Sauce

2 cups sugar creamed with ⅔ cup butter. Add 1 egg beaten light. When ready to serve add 1 cup of berries. Raspberries are just as good.

"Steamed Chocolate Pudding"

1 tablespoon butter and ½ cup sugar creamed together. ½ cup milk, 1 egg, 1 cup flour, 1 teaspoon baking powder, 2 squares chocolate. Steam 1 hour.

Hard Sauce

Cream together 4 tablespoons butter, 8 tablespoons powdered sugar. Add beaten white of egg. Flavor with Vanilla

"Lemon Sauce"

Boil ⅓ cup sugar ½ cup water 5 min., add 2 teaspoons butter, 1 teaspoon lemon juice, dash of nutmeg.

"Pineapple Meringue Pie"

1 can grated pineapple, 2 well beaten yolks of eggs, 2 tablespoons corn starch. Cook in double boiler till thick. Bake crust and put in filling. Cover with meringue made of 2 whites of egg beaten stiff, with 2 tablespoons powdered sugar. Brown lightly

"Lemon Sauce No. I."
¾ cup sugar — ¼ cup water
2 teaspoons butter — 1 Tablespoons Lemon Juice
Make a syrup by boiling
sugar and water 5 minutes;
remove from fire; add butter and
lemon juice.

"Hard Sauce"
⅓ cup butter   1 cup powdered sugar
¼ cup granulated sugar
⅓ teaspoon lemon extract
⅓ teaspoon vanilla
Cream butter and add sugar
gradually, while beating constantly,
then add flavoring.

Squash Pie
One cup squash, 1 pint milk, 3 crackers
rolled & sifted, ⅔ cup sugar, ½ teasp.
ginger ½ teaspoon cinnamon, ⅔ teasp.
salt. Mix squash, milk and cracker
crumbs together then add drys which
have been mixed together.

"Filled Chocolate Cookies"

One egg, 1 cup sugar, ½ cup shortening, 2 cups flour, ½ cup milk, 3 tablespoons cocoa, 1 teaspoon soda, 2 teaspoons cream tartar, fill and cover and bake.

Filling— One cup cocoanut, ½ cup milk, ½ cup sugar, 1 teaspoon flour. Cook until thick and cool.

Sour Milk Doughnuts

1 egg, 3/4 cup sugar, 1 tablespoon shortening
1/4 teaspoon salt, shaking each of nutmeg
& cinnamon, 3/4 cup thick sour milk
3/4 teaspoon soda, dissolved in milk,
2 1/2 to 3 cups flour sifted with 1/4 teasp.
baking powder. Mix in order given
having dough quite soft, kneading
in more flour on board if necessary

Marjie

Johnny Cake

Graham Muffins
1 cup flour   1 cup graham flour
1 egg   pinch of salt
2 spoonfuls sugar 1 spoonful cream tartar
1-2 spoonful soda 1 cup sweet milk
     Bake in hot oven. Makes 1 doz. muffins.
          "Johnny Cake"
  Cream 3/4 cup sugar and 1/4 cup butter. Add
1 beaten egg and beat again. Add 1 cup sour
milk in which 1 level teaspoon soda has
been dissolved. 1 cup Indian meal & 1 cup flour.
Beat well and bake about 25 minutes.

"Salad Dressing"

Scald ½ pt. of milk, and add ½ tablespoonful
of salt. ½ cup of sugar, 1 tablespoon
of flour, 1 tablespoon mustard,
butter the size of an egg and 1 egg.
After this has thickened add ½ cup
of vinegar.

"Meat Salad"

Cold meat, chopped fine, covered with
mayonnaise dressing and decorated
rings of hard boiled eggs and parsley
make a delicious supper salad when
on nice crisp lettuce leaves.

"Scotch Potatoes"

1 qt. potatoes   1 qt. onions   1 teasp. salt

Cut potatoes & onions and boil till
tender. Drain and put into a dish
and cover with thick cream sauce.
Bake in hot oven 25 min. Before baking
sprinkle top with grated cheese.

" Mrs. Ethel Wilson's Butter Scotch Pudding"
2 tablespoons flour – 2 tablespoons butter
Pinch of salt – Put into double
boiler and melt together. 3/4 cup light
brown sugar – stir into a pint of
warm milk – add yolk of 2 eggs – Cook
10 minutes.

"Alice Lemon Pie"
Grate

"Coffee Tapioca"
2 cups coffee or postum
3 rounding tablespoons tapioca
1/2 cup sugar – pinch of salt – 1 teasp. vanilla
Cook 15 min. in double boiler

"Strawberry Short Cake"
2 cups flour – 2 teaspoons sugar
4   ..   baking powder
1/2   ..   ..   salt
Sift all together then work in with
fingers 1/4 cup of butter, then add 1 cup
sweet milk – handle as little as
possible bake in two tins – when done
butter and add strawberries or any fruit.
Divide dough as nearly in half as can,
dip in flour and pat in tins to bake.
Do not roll it out.

Gingerbread

⅓ cup lard   ½ teasp. soda
½ cup sugar   1 teasp. baking powder
½ cup molasses   1 teasp. cinnamon
2 eggs   ½ .. salt
½ cup water   1½ cups flour
        1 cup cocoanut

Cream lard, add sugar, add beaten
eggs and molasses & beat well. Mix
& sift dry, add alternately with
water to first mixture. Fold in
cocoanut. Bake moderate oven 30 & 35 min.

Butter Pie

1 pint milk heated (Put in butter size of an egg
Mixed) rounded half cup sugar
1 tablespoon flour
Pinch of salt 2 beaten eggs
Teaspoon Vanilla after Cooked.

Pie Crust

½ Cupful lard – ½ cup boiling water, Beat all together. 1½ heaping cups flour. Sifted with ¼ teaspoonful salt & ½ teaspoonful baking powder.

Squash Pie Filling

1 Cup sifted squash
½ " sugar, pinch of salt
1 egg, Cinnamon & Nutmeg, milk to fill plate.

"Alice Lemon Pie"

Grate the rind of 3 lemons & squeeze the juice of them to
2 cups sugar
3 eggs – Butter size of nutmeg
2 tablespoonful cornstarch
2½ cups of hot water
Beat eggs and cornstarch together – Cook until thick.

"Mrs. M____oy's Plain White Cake"

2 cups flour
1 Cup sugar – 3 teaspoonfuls Baking powder – salt. Sift all together – 1 egg in cup of milk – Pour ingredients Beat all together – 1 tablespoon melted butter and beat that in.

Cream Pie (baked crust

Put in double boiler
½ c sugar mixed with
3 heaping (t) cornstarch
adding 2 beaten egg yolks
& a pinch of salt. add 2 cups
hot milk slowly stirring until it thicken
cool & flavor with vanilla
use the beaten whites to frost !
Cocoanut sprinkled on top makes an
addition
4 teaspoon of sugar to the whites

"D'vinity Fudge"

Put 3 cups sugar in a saucepan, add ½ cup corn syrup (white preferred) and ½ cup water. Boil until it spin a thread. Now turn this slowly into the beaten whites of 2 eggs stirring constantly. Add 1 cup walnut meats (cut fine) and 1 teaspoon Vanilla. Beat till ready to pour into buttered tin.

"Fudge" (½ recipe to frost a cake)

Cook 3 cups sugar, 1 cup milk, 1 tablespo. butter, and 5 tablespoons cocoa together in a spider. Boil until it forms a soft ball when put in cold water. Take from fire, add 5 tablespoons marshmallow cream, beat until th

"Coffee Fudge"

2 cups sugar 1 cup strong coffee
½ oz. butter ¾ cup pecans or other nuts
½ teaspoon almond essence

Boil first 3 ingredients till a soft ball can be formed when dropped in cold water. Add nuts and beat till a creamy consistency. Add flavor and pour into a buttered tin.

"Chocolate Frosting"

Beat together 2 tablespoons butter. ½ cup powdered sugar, add 2 tablespoons of cream, 1½ squares chocolate (melted) add enough powdered sugar to make a smooth paste. Flavor with ⅛ teaspoon cinnamon or vanilla.

"Cream Frosting"

2⅓ cup milk   2 cups sugar
Butter size of an egg. Boil 15 min, beat till cool and flavor. Very good

"Filled Cookies"

1 cup sugar   ½ cup butter
1 egg   1 teaspoon Vanilla
½ cup milk   1   "   soda
2 teaspoons cream tartar 3½ cups pastry flour

Roll dough very thin – cut

Filling

1 cup seeded raisins   ½ cup sugar
½ cup water   1 tablespoon flour

Cook till thick, stirring constantly. Drop teaspoonful on a cookie and cover with another, pressing edges firmly together. Prick top with a fork and bake.

"Pineapple Delight"
1 can of pineapple cut in small pieces
10 cents worth of marshmallows, cut
in quarters.
    Put together and pour the juice
of the pineapple over them.
Then add ½ pt. of cream whipped stiff.
Juice of one orange.
        "Coffee Whip"
3 large tablespoons flour 4 tablesp. sugar
½ teaspoon salt   2 cups coffee
½   "   vanilla   Whites of 2 eggs
  Mix dry ingredients together thoroughly.
Moisten with little ~~sugar~~ coffee, then
add remainder of coffee slowly, mixing
all smooth. Cook till thick stirring
often. Remove from stove, add flavor
Beat until spongy. Beat egg whites very
stiff, stir lightly into mixture. Set
away to cool. Serve with whipped
cream.
        "Strawberry Pudding"
½ cup sugar   1 cup milk
2 " flour   2 teaspoons melted butter
2 teaspoons baking powder. 1 egg
1 cup strawberries. Mix ingredients, flour
and baking powder sifted together.
    Steam 1 hour.   (cont)

"Butter Scotch Sauce for Ice Cream"

1¼ cups brown sugar
⅔ cup corn syrup
4 Tablespoons butter
⅞ cup heavy cream
⅜ cup milk

Put sugar, corn syrup and butter in sauce pan, bring to the boiling point and let boil until a soft ball may be formed when tried in cold water, then add cream and milk.

"Lemon Sauce n. F."

½ cup sugar
1 cup boiling water
1 Tablespoon Cornstarch
2 Tablespoons Butter
1½ Tablespoons lemon juice
Few gratings nutmeg

Mix sugar and cornstarch, add cold water gradually, stirring constantly. Boil 5 minutes, remove from fire, add butter, lemon juice and nutmeg.

Make "Vanilla Sauce" the same way using Vanilla instead of lemon and not use any nutmeg.

"Mother Earle's Lemon Pie"

Grate rind of two lemons and squeeze juice into 2 cups sugar, 3 eggs, butter size nutmeg, 3 tablespoons cornstarch, 2½ cup hot water. Beat eggs & cornstarch together. Cook till thick. Lemon rind can be omitted.

"Lemon Custard Pie"

1 cup sugar, 1 tablespoon flour, 2 eggs, 1 cup milk, juice of 1 lemon. Beat the whites of the eggs and add them last. Fold them in and bake in one crust. Very nice for hot weather.

"Coffee Cookies"

One cup sugar, 1 cup shortening, 1 cup cold, strong coffee, 1 cup molasses, 1 teaspoon cream tartar, 2 full teaspoons soda, a little salt, cloves and cinnamon to suit taste and flour to roll.

"Pop Overs"

Sift 1 teaspoon baking powder in one
pint flour. Add 1 well beaten egg and
1 large cup of milk and a little salt.
Bake in gem pan.

"Gems"

Cream together 2 tablespoons butter,
3 tablespoons sugar + 1 egg. 2 cups
flour, 1 teaspoon cream tartar,
½ teaspoon cream~~ soda~~ tartar sifted
in the flour.

Add 1 cup milk. Bake in iron
gem pan in quick oven.

"Surprise Muffins"

1¾ cups flour, 3 teaspoons baking powder
½ teaspoon salt, ¾ cup milk, 1½ tablespoons
butter, 1 egg, 1½ tablespoons sugar.
Bake in moderate oven about 30 min

"Pop Overs" II

1 egg, 1 cup milk, 1 cup flour, ½ teaspoon
salt. Mix + sift flour and salt. Beat egg
add milk, and add gradually to dry
mixture, making a smooth batter. Beat
with egg beater till mixture is full
of air bubbles. Bake in hot oven for
about 30 minutes.

"Creamed Cod Fish"

Cook 2 tablespoons flour in 2 tablespoons
butter. When bubbling pour in slowly
1 pint milk & cook (stirring constantly)
until smooth & thick - Add 2 cups of
flaked codfish - 2 chopped hard boiled
eggs - 1 tablespoon grated cheese - ½ cup
shredded green peppers - & 2 well beaten
eggs - season with salt - Cook thoroughly
serve on toast.

"Hamburg Loaf with Quaker Oats"

1 lb. hamburg steak - 1 egg - 1 scalded milk
¾ cups of quaker oats - 1 teaspoon Poultry
seasoning - 1 onion chopped fine - 1½
teaspoon salt.

"Macaroni & Tuna Fish Salad"

Cook macaroni until tender, cut very
fine, add as much dried celery or
shredded lettuce, a can of Tuna Fish.

"Sandwich Filling"

1 ten cent bottle stuffed olives
1 five cent cream cheese
¼ Spanish onion
1 hard boiled egg

Put through meat grinder and serve
as wanted with saltines.

"Apple Lemon Pie"

1 cup chopped apple – 1 cup sugar – 1 egg – juice & grated rind of 1 lemon – stir together sugar – egg & juice & rind of lemon – Line a plate with crust & pour apple into it – spread the mixture over apple and put on a top crust. Bake very slowly.

"Pineapple Cream"

1 cup rice – Washed & cleaned – 1 can grated pineapple. 1 Jar of heavy cream whipped – Cook rice in salt water until tender – when cool fold in 1 can grated pineapple. sweeten to taste & mix well – now mix in ½ pt. of cream whipped & serve cold.

"Apple Sauce Cake"

1 cup thick hot apple sauce – ½ cup melted butter, 1 cup sugar. When cool sift in 1½ cups flour to which has been added 1 teaspoon soda, stir in 1 cup chopped raisins – ½ teaspoon all kinds of spices and ½ cup chopped nuts.

"Jenny Ray's Sponge Cake"

4 eggs – whites & yolks beaten separate –
Then beaten together until light –
Pinch of salt – 1 cup of sugar beaten
into the eggs. Two tablespoons of
cold water with extract – Fold in
1 cup of flour – Cook in moderate oven.

"Edith Leonard Chocolate Cake"

2 squares chocolate or the equiv. (2 heaping
tablespoons of cocoa) Pour in ½ cup
boiling water 1 tablespoon butter –
1 cup sugar – 1 egg – ⅓ cup sour milk
1 small teaspoon of soda, dissolved
well in the sour milk. Pinch of
salt – 1 heaping cup of pastry flour.
1 teaspoon of vanilla – Bake in moderate oven

"E. L. Chocolate Custard Pie"

1 Pint milk
4 tablespoons sugar – 3 eggs – Pinch of salt
2   "   cocoa or 1 sq. of chocolate
1 teaspoon vanilla – Beats yolks of
eggs & add sugar & salt – Wet cocoa
with ½ cup of warm milk – stir into
the milk – Flavor – Line a deep pie
plate with crust – Pour mixture and
bake until rises – Beat the whites until
stiff froth – add 2 tbsps. sugar, spread & brown.

REVISED & REVIVED
Recipes and Recollections

Gram's Merriam Street kitchen

Cakes of All Kinds

Mother Earle's Sour Milk Spice Cake

Mother Earle's Sour Milk Spice Cake

1 extra-large egg, at room temperature
1 cup of sugar
½ cup of melted shortening
1 cup of sour milk
1 teaspoon of baking soda
¼ teaspoon each of cinnamon, cloves, and nutmeg
2 cups of all-purpose flour

Preheat the oven to 350 degrees. Grease a 9 x 5-inch loaf pan with shortening and dust with flour.

Sift the flour and spices together. Set aside.

To make the sour milk, take a liquid measuring cup and put in 1 tablespoon of vinegar or lemon juice. Add whole milk to equal 1 cup, and let the mixture sit at room temperature for 5 minutes. Add the baking soda to this mixture, and give it a quick stir with a whisk or fork.

In the bowl of an electric mixer, beat the egg until lemon-colored. Add the sugar and beat together for 1 minute. With the mixer running, slowly beat in the melted shortening until well incorporated. Add the flour and spices alternately with the milk mixture, beginning and ending with dry ingredients.

Spoon the batter into the prepared loaf pan, and bake until a wooden toothpick inserted in center comes out clean, about 1 hour. Remove from the oven and let cool for 10 minutes, then turn out onto a wire baking rack to cool completely. Serve with warm cinnamon applesauce (homemade, chunky style preferred) and sweetened whipped cream.

Cinnamon Applesauce: Peel, core, and slice 6 to 8 McIntosh or Granny Smith Apples (or a combination of the two). Place in a 3-quart saucepan along with ½ cup of apple juice, a stick of cinnamon, and a tablespoon of butter. Bring to a boil over high heat, then lower the heat to simmer and cover the pan with a lid. Cook the apples for about 20 to 25 minutes or until soft and mushy. Remove the pan from the stove. Discard the cinnamon stick and add a ¼ teaspoon of ground cinnamon, a dash of nutmeg, and a ¼ cup of light brown sugar. Mash the apples with a potato masher or fork until desired consistency.

*Lizzie (Mother) Earle pictured here
with her children Hazel, Vera, and Edward*

Edward and Arline (Knox) Earle

*Their children: Marjorie (my mother),
Robert, and Betty*

Other than being Gram's first mother-in-law, I don't know much about the role Lizzie Earle played in Gram's life. However, my mother has fond memories of Lizzie as a loving grandmother who was a tiny, quiet woman, always busy. My mother said she spent one of the best years of her life in the company of this lady who made the best gingersnap cookies and homemade biscuits.

Marjorie Earle, Lizzie Earle, and Robert Earle

Earle Gingerbread

It is interesting that this was called gingerbread, as there was no ginger listed in the ingredients. A moist cake with a strong molasses flavor, it is delicious with a cup of hot tea.

½ cup of sugar
½ cup of molasses
1 extra-large egg, beaten
1 tablespoon of unsalted butter, melted
1 cup of all-purpose flour
½ teaspoon of baking soda
¼ teaspoon each of ground nutmeg, cinnamon, and allspice
½ cup of boiling water

Preheat the oven to 350 degrees. Grease an 8 x 8-inch pan with shortening and dust with flour.

In the bowl of an electric mixer, beat together the sugar, molasses, and melted butter on medium speed for 1 minute. Add the egg, and beat for 1 minute more. Sift together the flour, baking soda, and spices. With the mixer on low, add the dry ingredients to the sugar mixture. Slowly add the boiling water, and mix until well blended. Pour into the prepared pan.

Bake for about 30 minutes. Place on a wire baking rack to cool slightly, cut into squares, and serve warm with whipped cream or lemon sauce.

Gingerbread (with lard)

Lard is rendered pig fat, and it was used in baked goods before the introduction of shortening in the 1930s. Don't be squeamish! You really must try this one! This gingerbread has a truly unique taste, and I love the addition of the coconut. Again, no ginger was listed.

⅓ cup of lard
½ cup of sugar
½ cup of molasses
2 extra-large eggs, lightly beaten
½ cup of water
½ teaspoon of baking soda
1 teaspoon of baking powder
½ teaspoon of cinnamon
½ teaspoon of salt
1½ cups of all-purpose flour
1 cup of shredded coconut

Preheat the oven to 350 degrees. Grease an 8 x 8-inch pan with shortening. Cream the lard and sugar together until well blended. Beat in the eggs and molasses.

Sift the dry ingredients, and add alternately with the water to the above mixture, beginning and ending with dry ingredients. Fold in the coconut. Pour into the prepared pan and bake for 30 to 35 minutes. Place on a wire baking rack to cool slightly, cut into squares, and serve warm with sweetened whipped cream.

Maurice "Sonny" Austin and Arline
(Knox) Earle, married on May 6, 1939

At the home they purchased on Merriam Street in Berwick, Maine, Gram and Sonny kept a menagerie of critters on the property: dogs, a cow, pigs, sheep, and even a pet skunk. The house was an old New Englander built in the 1800s, and was just down the road a piece from the ancestral farm where Gram was born and raised. It had a spooky attic with lots of treasures, and I was always finding reasons for Gram to take me up there to unearth a yet-unseen trinket from the boxes stored therein.

There was a long row of white metal cabinets and drawers in her pink-and-gray kitchen. The table and chairs sat in front of a double window that overlooked the backyard, where you could see a rhubarb patch tucked in behind the garage if the clothesline was free of shirts and "shorts." Pink scalloped shelves hung on either side of the window, displaying pieces of Gram's antique glassware and china, some of which had been passed down from family members.

Sadly, I don't have any stories of an apron-clad grandmother cooking feasts for me in this kitchen, although an aunt told me she used to cook three meals a day for Sonny. I guess it was a routine that died along with him.

But I do have memories of tea and treats. Gram used to buy this tea called "Boston's Mint-in-Tea" that came in a decorative tin, and I always looked forward to sipping a cup when Ma and I would drive to Berwick for a visit. There was a deep cupboard drawer right next to my seat at the table which contained Little Debbie treats, and I was always anxious to see whether crème-filled cakes or oatmeal crème pies were waiting for me.

On the days when the sun was strong and brandishing its warmth, we would take our tea out to the westward-facing front porch, and I would sway back and forth on Gram's gliding couch, relishing my lone treat and listening to family gossip.

Arline and Sonny's Merriam Street home

Angel Gingerbread

This gingerbread is light as a cloud.

½ cup of sugar
¼ cup of unsalted butter, at room temperature
1 extra-large egg, at room temperature
¼ cup of molasses
1 heaping cup of all-purpose flour
¼ teaspoon of cinnamon
1 teaspoon of ground ginger
½ cup of boiling water
1 teaspoon of baking soda

Preheat the oven to 350 degrees. Grease an 8-inch round cake pan with shortening and dust with flour.

In the bowl of an electric mixer, cream together the butter and sugar until light and fluffy. Beat in the egg and molasses. With the mixer on low, add the flour, cinnamon, and ginger.

Dissolve the baking soda into the boiling water and add to the above mixture until well combined. Pour into the prepared pan and bake for 30 to 35 minutes. Place on a wire baking rack to cool slightly, cut into squares, and serve with fresh whipped cream or a lemon sauce.

Applesauce Cake

This is one of the best applesauce cakes I've ever eaten.

1 cup of unsweetened applesauce
½ cup of melted unsalted butter
1 cup of sugar
1 extra-large egg, at room temperature
1½ cups of all-purpose flour
1 teaspoon of baking soda
1 teaspoon of pumpkin pie spice
1 cup of chopped raisins
½ cup of chopped walnuts

Preheat the oven to 350 degrees. Butter (use unsalted) and flour an 8 x 8-inch baking pan.

Warm the applesauce in a saucepan over low heat. Add the melted butter and sugar. Remove the pan from the heat, and quickly beat in the egg.

Sift the dry ingredients together. Add the chopped raisins and gently stir (this will ensure even distribution of the raisins in the cake batter, and keep them from settling to the bottom). Add the flour and raisins to the applesauce mixture. Gently stir in the walnuts. Pour the batter into the prepared pan and bake for 25 to 30 minutes. When completely cooled, dust with confectioners' sugar, cut into squares, and serve.

Maple Syrup Cake

This extremely moist and dense cake should be served with Maple Whipped Cream.

½ cup of shortening
½ cup of sugar
1½ cups of pure maple syrup
½ teaspoon of cinnamon
¼ teaspoon of ground cloves
¼ teaspoon of freshly ground nutmeg
1 teaspoon of baking soda
Pinch of salt
2 cups of all-purpose flour
1 cup of buttermilk
2 extra-large eggs, beaten

Preheat the oven to 350 degrees. Grease an 8 x 8-inch baking pan with shortening and dust with flour.

Beat the shortening and sugar together until creamy. Add the syrup and mix well. Sift together the dry ingredients, and add to the creamed mixture alternately with the buttermilk. Add the eggs and beat until well incorporated. Pour into the prepared pan and bake for 40 to 45 minutes or until a toothpick inserted in the center comes out clean. Place on a wire baking rack to cool completely. Cut into squares and serve with Maple Whipped Cream.

To make the Maple Whipped Cream, whip 1 pint of heavy cream and 1 to 2 tablespoons of maple syrup until firm but fluffy.

Chocolate Cake

This favorite is a nice little cake that's perfect for company.

¼ cup of unsalted butter, at room temperature
1 cup of sugar
1 extra-large egg, at room temperature
1 teaspoon of vanilla
½ cup of water
1½ cups of all-purpose flour
1½ teaspoons of baking powder
½ teaspoon of salt
2 heaping tablespoons of unsweetened cocoa

Preheat the oven to 350. Butter (use unsalted) and flour an 8 x 8-inch baking pan.

In a medium bowl, cream the butter and sugar until well combined. Add the egg, and beat for 1 minute. Add the vanilla, and beat for 30 seconds. In another bowl, sift the flour, baking powder, salt, and cocoa together. Add alternately to the creamed mixture with the water, beginning and ending with the dry ingredients.

Pour into the prepared pan and bake for 25 minutes, or until a toothpick inserted in the center comes out clean. Cool in the pan for 10 minutes, then remove to a wire baking rack to cool completely. Ice with the following frosting:

Frosting
Take an icing spatula and smooth this silky frosting over the top of the cake, letting it ooze down over the sides.

1½ tablespoons of unsalted butter, softened
2 cups of confectioners' sugar
1½ teaspoons of unsweetened cocoa
4 to 5 tablespoons of hot milk

Sift together the cocoa and confectioners' sugar. Place in the bowl of an electric mixer, and add the softened butter. Cream together with the mixer on low speed until well combined, and then add the hot milk 1 tablespoon at a time. Increase the mixer speed to high, and beat until the mixture is smooth. Spread over the cooled cake.

Edith Leonard's Chocolate Cake Intensified

My addition of espresso powder intensifies the original version, giving it a deeper, richer flavor. This cake is so good that it only needs a dusting of confectioners' sugar for presentation.

½ cup of unsweetened cocoa
2 tablespoons of unsalted butter, at room temperature
1 teaspoon of instant espresso powder
½ cup of boiling water
1 cup of sugar
1 extra-large egg, at room temperature
⅓ cup of buttermilk
½ teaspoon of baking soda
Pinch of salt
1 cup of cake flour
1 teaspoon of vanilla

Preheat the oven to 350 degrees. Grease an 8-inch round cake pan with shortening and dust with flour.

In a liquid measuring cup, whisk together the buttermilk and the baking soda, and set aside.

In a large bowl, combine the cocoa, butter, and espresso powder. Pour the boiling water over them, and stir until the butter is melted. Beat in the sugar and egg. Add the buttermilk mixture, along with a pinch of salt. Sift the flour and fold into the batter, then add the vanilla.

Pour into the prepared pan and bake for approximately 40 minutes. Cool in the pan for 10 minutes, then remove to a wire baking rack to cool completely.

Note: I had buttermilk and cake flour on hand, so I substituted these for the sour milk and pastry flour in the original recipe. The end result was a moist, flavorful chocolate cake.

Delicious Chocolate Cake

This is a nice, easy recipe, requiring only a few utensils and one pan. This would be a great recipe for a child to try (with supervision, of course).

½ cup of whole milk
1 rounded teaspoon of baking soda
½ cup of whole milk
2 ounces of unsweetened chocolate
⅓ cup of unsalted butter
1 cup of sugar
1 teaspoon of vanilla
1½ cups of all-purpose flour

Preheat the oven to 350 degrees. Grease an 8-inch round cake pan with shortening and dust with flour.

Combine the first ½ cup of milk in a liquid measuring container with the baking soda and set aside.

Place the other ½ cup of milk and the chocolate in a medium saucepan, and stir over medium-low heat until the chocolate is melted and the mixture starts to thicken. Remove the pan from the heat and add the butter, stirring until it is melted. Whisk in the sugar and vanilla until smooth. Stir in the milk/baking soda mixture until well incorporated. Carefully stir in the flour, and beat until the batter is smooth. Pour into the prepared pan, and bake for 25 to 35 minutes. Cool in the pan for 10 minutes, then remove to a wire baking rack to cool completely.

Mrs. Mahoney's Plain White Cake

Critics agreed that this is a slightly sweet "plain" cake that does not require any heavy frostings. Ideas for you to try: dust with confectioners' sugar and serve with fresh berries, or my favorite, caramelized pineapple chunks and sweetened whipped cream. YUM!

2 cups of all-purpose flour
1 cup of sugar
2 teaspoons of baking powder
⅛ teaspoon of salt
1 extra-large egg
1 cup of whole milk
2 tablespoons of melted unsalted butter

Preheat the oven to 350 degrees. Grease an 8-inch round cake pan with shortening and dust with flour.

Sift together the dry ingredients into a large mixing bowl. In a separate bowl, whisk together the egg and milk, and stir into the dry ingredients. Add the melted butter, and mix until the batter is smooth (about 30 seconds).

Pour into the prepared pan, and bake for about 40 minutes. Cool in the pan for 10 minutes, then remove to a wire baking rack to cool completely.

Caramelized Pineapple Chunks: In a medium non-stick skillet, melt 3 tablespoons of unsalted butter over medium heat. Add ¼ cup of light brown sugar and stir until sugar is dissolved. Add to this mixture, 1 cup of diced fresh pineapple. Cook and stir until the pineapple is heated through and turns a nice caramel color.

Jenny Ray's Sponge Cake

Once this cake is completely cooled, simply dust with confectioners' sugar, or split the cake in half and spread cherry jam in between the two layers. Serve with your favorite brand of coffee or tea.

4 extra-large eggs, at room temperature
Pinch of salt
1 cup of sugar
2 tablespoons of cold water
1 teaspoon of vanilla
1 cup of cake flour

Preheat the oven to 350 degrees. Grease a 9-inch round cake pan with shortening and dust with flour.

Separate the eggs and beat in separate bowls, beating the egg yolks until light and the whites to soft peaks.

Add the beaten egg whites to the beaten egg yolks, and mix at high speed until a light lemon color. Slowly add the sugar, and continue beating until the sugar has dissolved. Lower the speed to medium, and add the water and vanilla. Mix for 1 minute.

Sift the cake flour into a separate bowl, and with a spatula, fold by hand into the batter. Pour into the prepared pan, and bake for 30 to 35 minutes. Cool in the pan for 10 minutes, then remove to a wire baking rack to cool completely.

Frostings

All of these recipes yield about one cup, or enough to frost a small cake.

Butter

Beat together 2 tablespoons of whole milk, ¼ cup of softened unsalted butter, and 1 to 2 cups of confectioners' sugar (add just enough sugar to make mixture spreadable). Add ½ teaspoon of vanilla and beat well.

Mocha

Sift together 1 cup of confectioners' sugar and 2 teaspoons of unsweetened cocoa. Beat together with 2 tablespoons of room-temperature unsalted butter. Slowly beat in 2 tablespoons of boiling coffee, 1 tablespoon at a time, then add 1 teaspoon of vanilla.

Brown Sugar

In a 1-quart saucepan, stir together 1 cup of packed light brown sugar and 2 tablespoons of hot water. Over medium heat, bring to a boil, and boil vigorously for 2½ minutes. Meanwhile, in a medium bowl, beat the whites of 2 eggs until stiff peaks form. Slowly pour the hot sugar mixture over the egg whites, while beating on high speed. Beat until it reaches a spreadable consistency, and stir in ⅓ teaspoon of vanilla.

Chocolate I

I reduced the chocolate from the original recipe to give this frosting a lighter flavor and did not add the cinnamon.

Beat together 2 tablespoons of unsalted butter, ½ cup of sifted confectioners' sugar, 2 tablespoons of milk or cream, and one 1-ounce square of melted and cooled unsweetened chocolate. Add just enough additional sifted confectioners' sugar to make a smooth but firm consistency. Stir in ½ teaspoon of vanilla.

Chocolate II

In the top of a double boiler, melt two 1-ounce squares of unsweetened chocolate over medium-low heat. Add ¾ cup of sifted confectioners' sugar and 3 tablespoons of milk. Cook until the sugar is melted and the mixture is smooth. Take a bit of the mixture and whisk it into 1 beaten egg yolk; return to pan and whisk until well combined. Cook for 2 minutes. Remove from the heat and cool about 3 minutes, stirring once or twice. Pour and spread over a cooled cake. This is like a good chocolate ganache, smooth and velvety.

Muffins & Such

Rosemary Asiago Gems

Surprise Muffins

I couldn't quite figure out what the surprise was in these muffins until I did some research, and found similar recipes that listed the addition of jam or jelly baked in the middle of the batter, thus yielding a "surprisingly" sweet center. (The original recipe did not list the surprise ingredient of jam or jelly.) I tried it this way with much success, and added extra butter and sugar along with some canola oil. The final result was a moist muffin that had a richer flavor and golden color.

1 ¾ cups of all-purpose flour
3 teaspoons of baking powder
½ teaspoon of salt
3 heaping tablespoons of sugar
¾ cup of whole milk
3 tablespoons of unsalted butter, melted
¼ cup of canola oil
1 extra-large egg, at room temperature
Your favorite jelly or jam

Preheat the oven to 400 degrees. Using a 12-cup muffin tin, grease 8 of the cups with unsalted butter.

In a medium bowl, whisk together the flour, baking powder, salt, and sugar. Whisk together the melted butter, milk, oil, and egg. Stir into the dry ingredients.

Place about 2 tablespoons of batter in each muffin tin. Top with 1 teaspoon of jam or jelly. Top with remaining batter, equally divided. Sprinkle the tops with a little cinnamon-and-sugar mixture and dot with unsalted butter. Bake for 15 minutes or until golden brown, and serve hot from the oven.

Graham Muffins

Many of the recipes that I researched for this type of muffin called for a bit of molasses in the list of ingredients. After several attempts and as many failures to make a more edible version than the original, I decided to give the addition of molasses a try. It gave the muffins a rich brown color and the delectable sweetness that I was looking for.

1 cup of all-purpose flour
1 cup of graham flour
¼ cup of sugar
Pinch of salt
1 teaspoon of cream of tartar
1 teaspoon of baking soda
1 extra-large egg, at room temperature
1 cup of whole milk
¼ cup of unsalted butter, melted
3 tablespoons of molasses

Preheat the oven to 400 degrees. Using a 12-cup muffin tin, grease 9 of the cups with unsalted butter. In a large bowl, sift the dry ingredients. In a separate small bowl, whisk the egg, milk, butter, and molasses. Add this mixture to the dry ingredients, stirring until combined.

Divide the batter equally among the muffin cups, and bake for about 10 to 15 minutes. Place on a wire baking rack to cool slightly, then serve warm, slathered with butter!

Gems

An old New England favorite, gems were similar to muffins and were made in small cake tins. For my versions, I used a pre-seasoned cast-iron mini cake pan. I think these are fun to make, and you can come up with an endless variety of them. The next couple of pages include a few of my own.

The original recipe for Gems yielded a rather colorless and bland product. I added an additional two tablespoons of sugar and the lemon rind which gave them a more golden color, and a delicate tart flavor.

2 tablespoons of unsalted butter, at room temperature
4 tablespoons of sugar
1 extra-large egg, at room temperature
2 cups of all-purpose flour
1 teaspoon of cream of tartar
½ teaspoon of baking soda
1 cup of whole milk
Grated rind of one lemon

Preheat the oven to 425 degrees. Place a cast-iron mini cake pan in the oven to preheat while making the batter.

In the bowl of an electric mixer, cream the butter and sugar together. Add the egg, and beat for 1 minute.

Sift the flour with the cream of tartar and baking soda, and add to the butter, sugar, and egg mixture. With the mixer on low, pour in the milk, being careful not to over mix. Gently stir in the lemon rind.

Remove the heated pan from the oven and generously grease with shortening or unsalted butter. (I use about ½ teaspoon in each section and as it melts, I use a pastry brush to coat the pan completely.)

Using an ice cream scoop, fill the pan with equal amounts of batter. Bake for 15 to 20 minutes or until golden brown. Serve warm, split, and slather with lots of butter.

Happy Retreat Gems

These are a tribute to the often nutty moments at Gram's cottage by the sea. Make them for a summer brunch served with a glass of sweetened iced tea.

4 tablespoons of unsalted butter, at room temperature
2 tablespoons of white sugar
2 tablespoons of light brown sugar
1 extra-large egg, at room temperature
1 cup of cake flour
1 cup of all-purpose flour
1 teaspoon of cream of tartar
½ teaspoon of baking soda
1 cup of shredded coconut, toasted
1 tablespoon of fresh lime juice
Grated rind of two limes
1 cup of whole milk

Preheat the oven to 425 degrees. Spread the coconut on a small cookie sheet, and toast for five minutes. Remove to a plate and cool.

Place a cast-iron mini cake pan in the oven to preheat while making the batter.

In a medium bowl, sift the flours, cream of tartar, and baking soda. Gently whisk in the lime rind. In the bowl of an electric mixer, cream the butter and sugars until light and creamy. Beat in the egg. With the mixer on low, alternately add the flour mixture and the milk, beginning and ending with the dry ingredients. Stir in the lime juice and coconut.

Remove the heated pan from the oven, and grease with shortening.

Using an ice cream scoop, fill the pan with equal amounts of batter, and bake for 15 to 20 minutes. Remove from the oven, and place gems on a wire baking rack to cool completely. Glaze with a mixture made of 1 cup of confectioners' sugar and 1 or 2 teaspoons of lime juice, and sprinkle with additional toasted coconut.

Gram on the beach

Gram's Happy Retreat cottage in Wells Beach, Maine (purchased by her and Sonny in 1961), is where I spent many a happy summer visit. When the tides permitted, hours were spent down on the beach with Gram donning her sunglasses and white Gilligan's hat (of *Gilligan's Island* fame), taking in the view of the French-Canadian men in their Speedo's. As I got older, these observations would include a lewd comment followed by her cute chuckle.

Gram's "cottage" was just that, a small one-story dwelling built in the 1920s with scrap materials. It had a great screened-in front porch where one could sit and inhale the marvelous sea air, while watching the comings and goings of the tourists and locals.

Furnishings for this summer haven included mismatched furniture and souvenirs, washed-up lobster buoys, and gifts and homemade ceramics that various family members had given her. Every year a child could find the same old games and paper dolls to play with. Gram had an old View-master with vintage photographs, and for years there was an old-time radio in the corner of the living room with a turntable on which to spin and listen to 78 rpm records during a rainy day.

Some of the furniture was rigged together with rope, and the mattresses on the beds were a bit lumpy. The wiring was far from being "up to code," and the fuse box hung on the wall over one of the guest beds. On the back porch there was a small icebox that had to be unplugged before using the hot water tank. "Just in case," Gram would say.

Held together with scraps just like the cottage, I don't remember more than a handful of outfits Gram wore in all the years I knew her. Her most famous trademark was her slippers. They were boot-style, preserved in duct tape. They may have been the very first adult pair she owned, for all I know. The most memorable thing about them was the sound they made on the linoleum floors late at night when she took her nocturnal trip to the bathroom. She never put a light on so as not to wake anyone, but in the darkness you would hear the *swish-swish* from the duct tape as she shuffled her way to the loo.

Gram's wardrobe and cottage may have been a far cry from Anne Klein and Pottery Barn, but those of us who were lucky enough to spend time with her in that abode by the sea relished every minute of it.

Mornings at the cottage were my favorite part of the day. Early morning hours at the ocean can be nippy, even in the summer, and Gram would be the first one up to start the ancient furnace. She always told her guests, "Stay in bed where it's warm until I get the place heated up." When it was toasty enough to throw off the covers, it would be time to get up and start planning the day while having breakfast on the back porch overlooking the marsh.

Meals were never fancy affairs when Gram was the cottage cook. We ate mostly beans and hotdogs or Franco-American spaghetti with hamburger, but one could always find her staples of root beer in the fridge, pecan sandies in the cookie jar, and ice cream cups in the freezer. As the years passed and I became a cook in my own right, Gram was all too happy to pass the chef duties over to me, and she'd do the dishes and clean up.

A basket of stockpiled goods from local restaurants, particularly McDonalds, made its rounds between kitchen counter and dining table. These items included: napkins, plastic knives and forks, packets of ketchup, sugar, and mustard, salt and pepper, oyster and saltine crackers, and the occasional Styrofoam cup emblazoned with an establishment's logo, which was repeatedly washed and reused. Next to the stove, a metal pantry cabinet had its prominent place in the kitchen where you could find decade-old spice containers. The closet on the back porch had a can of potato chips in it that bulged and looked ready to explode.

When I became the cottage cook, I tried to persuade Gram to replace these items, but she always swore that "those are still good"—so

I always brought my own.

Gram would see no sentimentality in parting with what might become a family heirloom, such as these recipes, but she couldn't seem to get rid of brown oregano or a can of botulism.

Maple Pecan Gems

Gram loved any confection that was maple flavored. Maybe it was her centuries-old New England roots, but whatever the reason, I think she would have approved of this creation.

3 tablespoons of unsalted butter, at room temperature
4 tablespoons of dark brown sugar, packed
1 extra-large egg, at room temperature
1 teaspoon of maple extract
2 cups of all-purpose flour
1 teaspoon of cream of tartar
½ teaspoon of baking soda
½ cup of chopped pecans
1 cup of whole milk

Preheat the oven to 425 degrees. Place a cast-iron mini cake pan in the oven to preheat while making the batter.

Sift together the flour, cream of tartar, and baking soda. Set aside. In the bowl of an electric mixer, cream the butter and brown sugar until light and creamy. Beat in the egg and maple extract. With the mixer on low, stir in the dry ingredients and chopped pecans. Slowly add the milk.

Remove the heated pan from the oven and grease with unsalted butter.

Using an ice cream scoop, fill the pan with equal amounts of batter and bake for 15 to 20 minutes. Remove gems from the pan and place on a wire baking rack to cool slightly. Serve warm with butter and a drizzle of maple syrup, or let them cool completely and decorate with a maple confectioners' glaze and a pecan half.

Rosemary Asiago Gems

These receive rave reviews every time I make them. Make sure you use fresh rosemary!

4 tablespoons of unsalted butter, at room temperature
1 tablespoon of sugar
1 extra-large egg, at room temperature
1 teaspoon of cream of tartar
½ teaspoon of baking soda
2 cups of all-purpose flour
1 cup of freshly grated Asiago cheese
1 tablespoon of fresh rosemary, finely chopped
1 cup of buttermilk

Preheat the oven to 425 degrees. Place a cast-iron mini cake pan in the oven to preheat while making the batter.

Sift together the cream of tartar, baking soda, and flour. Lightly stir in the rosemary and cheese. Set aside. In the bowl of an electric mixer, cream the butter and sugar until light and fluffy, then beat in the egg. Add the dry ingredients alternately with the buttermilk, beginning and ending with the dry ingredients.

Remove the heated pan from the oven and grease with unsalted butter.

Using an ice cream scoop, fill the pan with equal amounts of batter, and sprinkle with a little additional grated Asiago cheese. Bake for 15 to 20 minutes. Remove from the pan and place on a wire baking rack to cool. Serve at room temperature with your favorite pasta dish, a steaming bowl of minestrone soup, or a juicy roast chicken.

One bright summer day my friend Nanci came to visit and she brought me some beautifully fragrant rosemary from her garden. At the time, I was in the "revised" stage of recipe testing. Not sure of how I was going to utilize this woodsy herb, the next day I spotted a block of Asiago cheese in the fridge, and decided to combine its nutty flavor with the rosemary to create what has become a critically acclaimed recipe, Rosemary Asiago Gems.

How does this fit in with memories of Gram? Well, Gram loved my Italian cooking and since these ingredients are synonymous with that particular cuisine, they reminded me of a culinary faux pas I made in preparation of a Sunday dinner to which she was invited.

Go back about twenty years or so, and you are in the kitchen of the home I shared with my husband Tom and our two daughters, Andrea and Maria. Being concocted on the stove is a big pot of homemade spaghetti sauce that will be the topping for some baked stuffed shells for dinner.

In my big saucepot, the onions have been softened in olive oil to a nice translucent color, and the garlic has been added and sautéed just enough to release its aroma. Next I stir in the canned tomatoes and puree, and get ready to sprinkle in the seasonings. In goes the measured oregano, basil, parsley flakes, crushed red pepper flakes, salt, and black pepper. I need fennel, too, and there's only a small amount left in the plastic fennel seed container, so I just dump what's remaining onto the top of the sauce.

Just as I'm about to take my big wooden spoon and stir in all of these essential components, I notice things moving on top of the sauce. Pressed for time, panicking, and not having enough ingredients on hand to start over, I scrape everything I see moving out of the pot! I say a prayer, and hope that the heat and cooking process will kill whatever I might have missed.

It was not one of my proudest moments in the kitchen, and it was never to be repeated. The guilt haunts me to this day. However, it turned out to be one of the best batches of homemade sauce I have ever made—and Gram said so, too.

The dinner guest list varied from time to time, but if you requested her company, Gram never turned down an invitation. Below is a photo showing Gram sharing a feast with some of my husband's Italian family. It was Easter dinner, and the menu included homemade ravioli with bug-free sauce and baked ham.

From left to right: Louise, my mother-in-law,
my husband's Aunt Theresa, and Gram

Johnny Cake

Johnny Cake is cornbread—also known in some historical recipes as Journey Cake because it travelled well. This recipe makes a moist, sweet version.

¾ cup of sugar
¼ cup of unsalted butter, at room temperature
1 extra-large egg, at room temperature
1 cup of sour milk or buttermilk
1 teaspoon of baking soda
1 cup of fine cornmeal
1 cup of all-purpose flour

Preheat the oven to 425 degrees. Grease an 8 x 8-inch baking pan with shortening.

Add the teaspoon of baking soda to the sour milk or buttermilk, and set aside. Cream the sugar and butter together. Beat in the egg, then stir in the milk/soda mixture.

Sift the flour and combine with the cornmeal; add to the above. Pour into the prepared pan, and bake for 20 to 25 minutes or until a toothpick inserted in center comes out clean. Place on a wire baking rack to cool slightly, cut into squares, and serve warm with lots and lots of butter.

Sour Milk "Doughnuts"

As tempting as it is to eat these while still hot, they are better enjoyed when completely cooled.

1 extra-large egg, at room temperature
¾ cup of sugar
1 tablespoon of shortening, melted
¾ cup of sour milk
1 tablespoon of sour cream
¾ teaspoon of baking soda
¼ teaspoon of salt
¼ teaspoon of cinnamon
¼ teaspoon of nutmeg
¼ teaspoon of baking powder
3 cups of all-purpose flour
3-pound can of shortening for frying

In the bowl of an electric mixer, beat the egg and sugar together, then stir in the melted shortening.

Whisk the sour cream into the sour milk. Dissolve the baking soda in this mixture, and add to the butter, sugar, and shortening, stirring to combine.

Sift together the salt, spices, baking powder, and flour, and stir into the the above ingredients. Cover the bowl with plastic wrap or a clean kitchen towel, and let rest for about 10 minutes.

Turn onto a floured board and knead a few times. The dough will be soft and tacky, so kneading it with a little flour makes it easier to cut into shape, and prevents it from sticking to the board. Pat the dough to ½-inch thickness, and cut out all the donuts. Let them rest uncovered while melting and heating the shortening. (This allows them to form a slight crust, which cuts down on the amount of fat they absorb while frying.)

Place all but 1 cup of the 3-pound can of shortening in a 3-quart saucepan. Place a deep fry thermometer with an adjustable clip in the saucepan. The thermometer should not touch the bottom of the pan. Melt the shortening over medium heat and when the temperature reaches 350 degrees, take a couple of the donut holes and drop them in the hot fat, cooking them for about 1 to 2 minutes on each side. Remove from the hot fat with a strainer, and place on paper towels to drain. Cool slightly and roll in granulated sugar (optional).

Continue with the remaining donut holes and donuts. (Don't place more than 3 doughnuts in the pan at a time, as this will bring the temperature of the fat down and they won't cook evenly. Keeping the temperature at 350 degrees will let the donuts cook thoroughly, and prevent them from absorbing too much grease. This can be tricky with an electric stove, but just don't crowd the pan. If you see the temperature getting too hot, add some of the reserved shortening, and this will bring the temperature down slightly.)

This recipe makes approximately 1 dozen donut holes and a dozen donuts.

Sour Milk Donuts

There are two establishments that Gram introduced me to that resulted in an endless craving for donuts (thank goodness I don't always give in to such yearnings).

In Wells, Maine, there is a still-famous donut shop called Congdon's. When summer arrived and the lure of Gram's cottage beckoned you, your first trip of the season to the seaside oasis was not complete until you took a drive up Mile Road to purchase some of Congdon's donuts to bring back and relish on the back porch. A favorite among most guests was the Bavarian crème filled, but Gram always requested a butter crunch donut.

Another local favorite was Pearl's Bakery in Somersworth, New Hampshire. When my girls were in elementary school, Gram would show up at the house unexpectedly, just minutes before the school bus brought them home in the afternoon. The moment I saw her little blue Ford pull up in front of the house, I knew what was coming: maple squares! Not just any maple squares, but expertly-crafted, scrumptiously airy donuts filled with vanilla cream and topped with maple frosting from Pearl's. When my girls came through the front door and saw the familiar white box on the dining room table, their eyes would light up with excitement. As we sat devouring our squares, Gram would slowly savor hers down to every last finger-licking morsel. They were pillows of perfection, and even though Pearl's went out of business many years ago, their maple squares remain unrivalled.

Popovers

I had never eaten a popover before making this recipe. What was I waiting for? They are quick, easy, and delicious, and they make a great breakfast treat!

Preheat the oven to 425 degrees. Using a 12-cup non-stick muffin tin, grease 8 of the cups with melted unsalted butter. Sift together 1 cup of flour and ⅛ teaspoon of salt in a medium bowl. In another bowl, whisk together 1 extra-large egg, 1 cup of whole milk, and 1 teaspoon of melted unsalted butter. With an electric hand mixer, slowly beat the egg/milk mixture into the flour. Beat on high until mixture is smooth and full of bubbles. (You should see tiny bubbles throughout the batter.)

Using a small ladle, distribute the batter evenly among the 8 cups. Bake at 425 degrees for 20 minutes. Then turn the oven temperature down to 350 degrees and bake for another 10 to 15 minutes. Serve hot from the oven with butter and honey or molasses.

Popovers have a doughy middle which some people prefer to remove before devouring.

Cookies & Fudge

Filled Cookies

Filled Cookies

Pearl's Bakery in Somersworth, New Hampshire not only made those awesome maple squares I told you about, but they also made scrumptious date-filled cookies. When a jaunt with Gram took us within the vicinity of this amazing establishment, she and I would stop in and Gram would buy us each one of these sugary cookie delights. It was such a tease to only eat one; nonetheless, I was always appreciative. These cookies are a close second to those treasure-filled treats.

1 cup of sugar
½ cup of unsalted butter, at room temperature
1 extra-large egg, at room temperature
1 teaspoon of vanilla
1 teaspoon of baking soda
2 teaspoons of cream of tartar
3½ cups of pastry flour
½ cup of whole milk
1 beaten egg white (for brushing cookies prior to baking)

Preheat the oven to 375 degrees. Cream together the butter and sugar until light and fluffy. Add the egg and vanilla, and beat well. Combine the dry ingredients and add alternately with the milk, beginning and ending with dry ingredients. Form the dough into a ball, cover with plastic wrap, and refrigerate for a couple of hours. While the dough is being chilled, make the filling.

Filling
1 cup of chopped raisins
½ cup of sugar
1 tablespoon of flour
½ cup of water

In a 2-quart saucepan, whisk together the sugar and flour, then whisk in the water. Add the raisins and cook over medium heat until thick, stirring constantly with a wooden spoon. Set aside to cool completely.

Once the filling has thoroughly cooled, divide the dough into quarters. Roll one section at a time on a floured board to ⅛-inch thickness. Cut out rounds with a 2-inch cookie cutter.

Place a teaspoon of the filling on top of one round. Cover with another round, and press them together lightly around the edges. Brush the tops with a little beaten egg white and poke small holes in the top of each cookie with a fork. Place on an ungreased cookie sheet 2-inches apart, and bake for 9 minutes. Immediately remove cookies to a wire baking rack to cool. (They will stick to the pan if you don't!) Let them cool completely before consuming.

Bet you can't eat just one!

Coffee Cookies

This recipe makes a thin and not overly sweet cookie. They go perfectly with a cup of freshly brewed coffee. For a summer treat, make them into ice cream sandwiches: soften some coffee or vanilla ice cream and gently sandwich a scoop between two cookies. Wrap in plastic wrap and freeze. Viola! Frozen fun!

1 cup of sugar
1 cup of shortening
1 cup of molasses
1 extra-large egg, at room temperature
1 teaspoon of cream of tartar
2 teaspoons of baking soda
Pinch of salt
1 teaspoon of cloves
1 teaspoon of cinnamon
5 cups of all-purpose flour
1 cup of cold, strong coffee

Cream the sugar and shortening until light and fluffy. Stir in the molasses. Add the egg and beat well. Sift the dry ingredients together, and then add alternately with the cold coffee. Cover the bowl with plastic wrap and chill the dough for at least 3 hours or overnight.

When ready to bake, preheat the oven to 375 degrees. Working in small batches, roll the dough on a floured surface to a ⅛-inch thickness and cut into desired shapes. (I use a 2 ⅝-inch fluted cookie cutter.) Place on an ungreased cookie sheet 2 inches apart, and sprinkle with Demerara sugar. (Demerara is raw sugar that contains molasses and is often used to decorate cookies and desserts.)

Bake for 5 to 6 minutes. Remove from the oven and let rest on the cookie sheet for 1 or 2 minutes before removing to a wire baking rack to cool completely. This recipe makes about 6 to 7 dozen cookies.

Filled Chocolate Cookies

The dough for this cookie is extremely delicate, and a little hard to roll without excessive amounts of flour, but your patience will be rewarded. The first time I made these, I packaged them up nicely and stored them in the freezer for gifts. Only a few ever left my doorstep.

1 extra-large egg, at room temperature
1 cup of sugar
½ cup of shortening
2 cups of all-purpose flour
3 heaping tablespoons of unsweetened cocoa
1 teaspoon of baking soda
2 teaspoons of cream of tartar
½ cup of whole milk

Cream together the shortening and sugar until light and fluffy. Add the egg and beat well. Sift together the dry ingredients and add alternately with the milk, beginning and ending with the dry ingredients. Form the dough into a ball and wrap in plastic wrap. Refrigerate while preparing and cooling the filling.

Filling
1 cup of flaked coconut
½ cup of whole milk
½ cup of sugar
1 teaspoon of flour
1 tablespoon of spiced dark rum (optional)

Place all ingredients in a 2-quart saucepan and cook over medium heat, stirring constantly, until thick. Remove from the stove and cool to room temperature.

Preheat the oven to 375 degrees. Remove the dough from the refrigerator. Working with a small batch of dough at a time, roll to ⅛-inch thickness on a floured board, and cut into 2-inch rounds using a cookie cutter. Place one round on an ungreased cookie sheet. Top with a generous teaspoon of the filling. Top with another round. Press the edges together lightly with your fingers. Gently brush cookies with a pastry brush to remove any excess flour. (This will result in a more attractive cookie.)

Bake for 11 minutes, and remove immediately from the cookie sheet to a wire baking rack to cool. This recipe makes about 2 dozen cookies.

To make these extra-special, drizzle a thin confectioner's icing over the top of the cookies when they are completely cooled.

Gram and her beloved fudge from Santa

Fudge was the ultimate treat for Gram, and I was disappointed that of the three fudge recipes that were rescued, I could only master making "Divinity." Trying to make "Fudge" and "Coffee Fudge" from the original found recipes, cost me a small fortune and a test of my patience, and I finally gave up. Even after I purchased the ideal candy thermometer (one with a clip attached for the side of the saucepan) success was not in the cards.

My favorite attempt was when I jury-rigged a thermometer to the side of the saucepan with plastic clothespins! You know where this is going, don't you? I was using an old candy thermometer without one of those attachments, and wanting to have both hands free, I used Yankee ingenuity and "created" my own version with the plastic clothespins. When the ingredients had bubbled and reached the soft ball stage, I grabbed a potholder to remove the thermometer and clothespin from the scalding liquid, and the whole damn thing slipped and fell into the bubbling cauldron!

Swearing and quickly trying to decide what to use to fish it out, I watched with horror as the plastic clothespins started to melt in my beautifully cooked ingredients! Finally lifting out the melting clothespins and thermometer with a wide spatula, I plopped the whole coated mess onto the top of the stove where it immediately hardened and later had to be chipped off. As soon as the profanity stopped I did a deep belly laugh at my stupidity.

Divinity Fudge

Weather affects the outcome of this fudge, so don't make it on a cloudy day.

2 extra-large egg whites, at room temperature
3 cups of sugar
½ cup of light corn syrup
½ cup of water
1 teaspoon of vanilla

In a large bowl, beat the egg whites with an electric handheld mixer until they form stiff peaks.

In a 2-quart saucepan bring the sugar, light corn syrup, and water to a boil over medium heat, stirring constantly, until it starts to boil. Clip an adjustable candy thermometer to the side of the pan, making sure it does not touch the bottom. Continue boiling the mixture until it reaches the hard-ball stage, at 260 degrees. Remove the saucepan from the heat, unclip the thermometer, and with the mixer running on high, SLOWLY pour this mixture into the egg whites. (Do not scrape the pan.)

When the ingredients are well incorporated, add the vanilla. Continue beating at high speed for 1 to 2 minutes until the beaters leave ripples on the top. Pour immediately into a buttered 8 x 8-inch pan (do not scrape the bowl, just push the batter gently into the pan with a spatula). Let it cool and then cut into heavenly divine squares.

Puddings & Sauces

Strawberry Pudding

Gram with her signature purse

My first food memory associated with Gram involved a roll of the assorted Five-Flavor Life Savers candies.

When I was five years old, we lived in an apartment house up the street from Gram. My Dad was in the Navy, and his meager salary didn't allow for many frills in the food department. The only sweets we had in the house were canned fruit or Jell-O.

We saw Gram often, and when she came to our house to visit, she always had her buff-colored purse with her. I remember one visit in particular, because nestled inside that signature purse was a surprise package of those brightly-wrapped circles of delight for my sister, brother, and I to share. Those candies were the best thing to ever hit my tongue. I had never tasted anything so good! It was complete nirvana, and was the beginning of my lifelong love affair with sweets.

From the first day we set eyes on the Five-Flavor Life Savers, we were enthralled with Gram's purse. Its contents were never without a sugary treat for us grandkids, and it got even better when we were later introduced to Canada Mints, Necco Wafers, root beer barrels, and butterscotch candies. On special occasions, there was a small box of Whitman's chocolates, but the coup de grâce for me was the day she brought us a roll of Butter Rum Life Savers! Oh, how I loved that purse—and Gram too, of course!

Mrs. Ethel Wilson's Butterscotch Pudding

This is very sweet, but oh, so delish! This pudding is a cross between those butter rum and butterscotch flavors, and the first time I tasted it, I went right back to the days when such goodness was a rare treat. This is smooth and velvety, and if you love butterscotch pudding, you have to try it.

2 tablespoons of all-purpose flour
2 tablespoons of unsalted butter
Pinch of salt
¾ cup of light brown sugar
2 cups of warm milk
2 egg yolks, beaten

In the top of a double boiler over medium heat, melt the butter, and whisk in the flour and pinch of salt. Cook together for about 1 minute; then stir in the light brown sugar until well incorporated. Slowly whisk in the warm milk, and continue stirring until the sugar is dissolved. Temper the eggs with a little of the milk/sugar mixture. (Tempering means to whisk in a little of the hot mixture into the beaten eggs, then whisking the eggs into the pan. This warms the eggs so they don't turn into scrambled eggs when added to the hot pudding mixture.) Continue whisking for about 10 minutes, or until pudding thickens.

Pour the pudding through a strainer or sieve into a bowl, and spoon into serving dishes. Cover with plastic wrap. Cool slightly and place in refrigerator until well chilled. Serve with whipped cream.

Pineapple Cream

It was a test of will power not to devour this before it even made it to the fridge! You can use any rice you like, but Jasmine rice is great for puddings. Tahitian vanilla compliments the floral flavor of the rice. Used primarily in dishes that do not need to be cooked, it can be found in kitchen and food specialty stores.

1 cup of cooked and cooled Jasmine rice
1 8-ounce can of crushed pineapple (don't drain)
1 cup of heavy cream
4 tablespoons of confectioners' sugar
1 teaspoon of Tahitian vanilla

With an electric mixture, whip the heavy cream with the confectioners' sugar and vanilla until very stiff.

Combine the rice and pineapple, and gently fold into the whipped cream. Transfer to serving dishes or a pretty glass bowl, cover, and refrigerate. Serve very cold.

Steamed Chocolate Pudding

1 tablespoon of unsalted butter, at room temperature
½ cup sugar
2 1-ounce squares of unsweetened chocolate, melted and cooled
½ cup of whole milk
1 extra-large egg, at room temperature
1 cup of all-purpose flour
1 teaspoon of baking powder

Cream together the butter and sugar. Add the melted and cooled chocolate, and mix well. Whisk together the milk and egg, and add to the sugar/chocolate mixture. The mixture will look a little curdled. Sift together the flour and baking powder, and add to the other ingredients.

Pour the batter into a heavily buttered 1-quart mold, cover tightly with aluminum foil, and tie with a piece of butchers twine. Place a rack in a large stockpot and fill with about 4 inches of water. Bring the water to a boil over high heat. Carefully place the pudding/mold on the rack. Turn the heat down to low, cover the pot with a tight-fitting lid, and steam for 1 hour. (If you do not have a tight-fitting lid for the pot, cover tightly with foil.) The water should come up halfway on the side of the mold. Replenish the water, if needed, with boiling water to keep the steam bath temperature even.

The pudding is done when a toothpick inserted in the center comes out clean, about 1 hour. Remove from the pot, uncover, and let stand on a wire baking rack for 10 minutes. Unmold and serve warm with whipped cream, or in the traditional way, with a hard sauce. This makes a great dessert for company.

Strawberry Pudding

An incredibly awesome dessert! You have to try it to believe it! It is best made when strawberries are in season, which here in New England is June. However, it's also guaranteed to put a smile on the face of any cabin-fever victim on a cold winter day and bring back memories of a warm summer day.

½ cup of sugar
1 extra-large egg, at room temperature
2 teaspoons of melted butter
2 cups of all-purpose flour
2 teaspoons of baking powder
1 cup of whole milk
1 cup of fresh diced strawberries

Beat together the sugar and egg until lemon-colored. Add the melted butter, and beat until smooth. Sift together the flour and baking powder, and add alternately with the milk, beginning and ending with the dry ingredients. Fold in the strawberries.

Pour the batter into a heavily buttered 1-quart mold, cover tightly with aluminum foil, and tie with a piece of butchers twine.

Place a rack in a large stockpot and fill the pot with about 4 inches of water. Bring the water to a boil over high heat. Carefully place the pudding/mold on the rack. Turn the heat down to low, cover the pot with a tight-fitting lid, and steam for 1 hour. (If you do not have a tight-fitting lid, cover tightly with aluminum foil.)

The water should come halfway up the side of the mold. Replenish the water, if needed, with boiling water to keep the steam bath temperature even. Steam for about 1 hour and 20 minutes, or until a toothpick deeply inserted in center comes out clean. Remove from the pan, uncover, and invert onto a pretty plate. Serve with hot vanilla sauce and some additional sliced strawberries.

Sauces

Vanilla Sauce
½ cup of sugar
1 tablespoon of cornstarch
1 cup of cold water
2 tablespoons of unsalted butter
1½ tablespoons of vanilla bean paste

In a 2-quart saucepan, combine the sugar and cornstarch. Slowly stir in the cold water. Bring to a boil over high heat, stirring constantly. Turn heat down to medium high, and boil for 5 minutes. (You do not need to keep stirring at this point.)

Remove from the heat, and stir in the butter and vanilla bean paste. YUM!

Lemon Sauce
Make the same as Vanilla Sauce, except to replace the vanilla bean paste with 1½ tablespoons of lemon juice and a dash of nutmeg.

Hard Sauce
Cream ⅓ cup of unsalted butter. Slowly add 1¾ cup of sifted confectioners' sugar; adding a little at a time and beating well after each addition. Beat in ⅓ teaspoon of lemon extract and ⅔ teaspoon of vanilla. Beat until light and fluffy. Serve piled high in a pretty glass dish with your favorite steamed pudding.

On Route 1 in Ogunquit, Maine sat a popular ice cream parlor that sadly locked its doors for the last time many years ago. The Viking Ice Cream & Candies Shop was just a short drive from Gram's cottage in Wells, and as a child, once or twice a summer season she would take me there for an ice cream smorgasbord.

For a reasonable price, we would go up to the counter and order our ice cream: vanilla for me and butter pecan for Gram. A nice lady would set our scoop in a pretty glass sundae dish set atop a doily and saucer. We would then move down an assembly line of blissful toppings to choose from, starting with a choice of chocolate, hot fudge, or hot butterscotch sauce!

Gram and I *always* got the hot butterscotch, and we would pile on various toppings and complete our sundaes with whipped cream, nuts, and a cherry until it overflowed onto the saucer below. Gram made sure to get her money's worth, and we always went to the water cooler and got a little paper cup of water to "wash it all down," as Gram would say.

Why not invite family and friends over, have your own smorgasbord, and include the following delectable recipe for Butterscotch Sauce?

Butterscotch Sauce For Ice Cream

1¼ cups of brown sugar
⅔ cup of light corn syrup
4 tablespoons of unsalted butter
⅜ cup of heavy cream
⅜ cup of whole milk

Place the brown sugar, corn syrup, and butter in a 2-quart saucepan and bring to a boil, stirring constantly. Attach an adjustable candy thermometer to the pan, and boil the mixture until it reaches the soft-ball stage (234–240 degrees). Remove from the heat, and whisk in the heavy cream and milk. Serve hot from the pan on your favorite frozen flavor.

Pies

Pineapple Cocoanut Pie

I have a few words about making pies. First and foremost, make your own crust! For those who say they can't make a good pie crust, I say practice, practice, practice! There really is no comparison between a good homemade crust and those chemical-smelling, ready-made things you buy in the grocery store. Experiment with recipes using different fat content: shortening, butter, or lard. I've had luck with all three, but prefer crust made with shortening or lard.

Purchase yourself a stoneware or professional-grade pie pan. The results will be an evenly cooked crust (without the soggy bottom), which is essential to a good piece of pie. Also purchase a metal pie saver to prevent the edges of your crust from browning too much in the oven.

As with all baked products, use the best ingredients you can afford, and check your freshness dates before you begin.

Last but not least, when making meringue, use superfine sugar. It dissolves faster, and you will be less likely to get those moisture droplets on the surface of your meringue. Meringue shrinks as it bakes, so make sure you completely cover your pie filling by spreading the meringue almost to the edge of the crust if necessary.

A note on the pie recipes listed here: They were all made with a 9-inch pie crust, which will yield a sizeable amount of filling, but if you wish for a higher volume of pie filling, use an 8-inch pie crust/dish— just make sure to allow for extra cooking time.

Pie Crust

This recipe makes one 9-inch crust.

There is no need to let this dough rest, as there is with some pie-crust recipes. This is a delicate crust to work with, but I loved the warm, silky feel of the dough. For those not squeamish about using lard, you will be rewarded with a tender, flaky, and flavorful crust. Give it a try!

½ **cup of lard**
⅓ **cup of boiling water**
1½ **cups of all-purpose flour**
¼ **teaspoon of salt**
½ **teaspoon of baking powder**

In the bowl of a food processor, add the flour, salt, and baking powder, and pulse a few times to combine. Add the lard, and pulse until mixture looks like coarse crumbs. With processor running, slowly pour in the boiling water through the feed tube, and process until the mixture forms a ball.

Remove from the processor, and work the dough into a smooth ball; roll out on a floured board, and line a 9-inch pie plate.

Note: Sometimes rolling pie dough can be tricky. It depends on the recipe and possibly the weather, but I will share with you my favorite method, learned from my mother many moons ago.

Take a pastry board (or use the top of an impeccably clean counter) and moisten a large area slightly with water squeezed from a dishcloth. (Don't use too much, or the waxed paper will tear while you are rolling.) Place a large piece of waxed paper on top, pressing down to make a smooth surface. Place your pie dough on top, and cover with another large piece of waxed paper; roll to the size desired. Carefully peel off the top piece of waxed paper; invert dough into pie plate, and peel off the other piece of waxed paper. (Be careful when you do this, so you don't tear the pie dough.)

Lemon Custard Pie

1 cup of sugar
1 tablespoon of all-purpose flour
2 extra-large eggs, separated and at room temperature
1 cup of scalded whole milk, cooled slightly
Juice of one large lemon
9-inch unbaked pie crust

Preheat the oven to 350 degrees. In a large bowl, combine the sugar and flour, and beat in the egg yolks with an electric mixer. Slowly beat in the scalded milk until well combined and just slightly thickened; beat in the lemon juice.

In another large bowl, beat the egg whites until stiff; then fold into the above mixture. Pour into an unbaked 9-inch pie crust and bake for about 35 to 40 minutes, or until a knife inserted in the center comes out clean. Place on a wire baking rack to cool completely before serving. Refrigerate any leftovers.

Mother Earle's Lemon Pie

The original recipe says that the lemon rind can be omitted. Including the rind makes a very tart pie, and for those who like a milder punch of lemon, you might want to omit the rind.

Juice and rind of 2 lemons
2 cups of sugar
3 extra-large eggs, at room temperature
2 tablespoons of cornstarch
2½ cups of boiling water
1 teaspoon of salted butter
9-inch baked pie crust

Preheat the oven to 350 degrees. In a liquid measuring cup, whisk the eggs and cornstarch together. Set aside.

Combine the lemon juice and rind with the sugar in a 3-quart saucepan. Add the 2½ cups of boiling water and cook over medium-high heat, stirring constantly until slightly thickened. Remove the pan from the heat, and whisk a little of the hot mixture into the egg/cornstarch mixture. Whisk the egg mixture into the saucepan, and return to the heat. With a wooden spoon, cook and stir the pie filling until it becomes thick. Remove from heat, and stir in the butter.

I like to pour this through a sieve or colander over a bowl at this point to remove any bits of cornstarch that may not have dissolved. Let cool slightly. Pour into a 9-inch baked pie crust. Make a meringue (see page 94), spread over the lemon pie filling in the shell, and bake for about 15 minutes. Let cool on a wire baking rack, then place in refrigerator until thoroughly chilled.

Squash Pie I

During the prosperous years in the Smith household, Ma baked two pies for Thanksgiving: pumpkin and squash. A pumpkin pie would have been sufficient for our small crew, but she always included a squash pie on the menu because it was one of Gram's favorites. There were usually only one or two pieces of this pie left at the end of the day, and Ma always sent the remainder home with Gram. Our family is big on doggie bags for guests.

1 cup of cooked squash (See Note)
½ cup sugar
Pinch of salt
1 extra-large egg
½ teaspoon of cinnamon
½ teaspoon of nutmeg
1½ cups of whole milk
9-inch unbaked pie crust

Preheat the oven to 425 degrees.

Combine the squash, sugar, salt, egg, and spices in a bowl and whisk together. Stir in the whole milk.

Place the unbaked pie shell on the middle rack of your oven, and slowly and carefully pour the squash mixture into the shell. Bake the pie at 425 for 15 minutes; then reduce the temperature to 350 degrees and cook until a knife inserted in the center comes out clean, about 40 minutes. Place on a wire baking rack to cool. Serve with sweetened whipped cream. Store any leftovers in the refrigerator.

Note: To cook the squash: Take a butternut squash and cut it in half lengthwise. Remove the seeds. Place both halves flesh side down on a cookie sheet lined with foil. Bake at 375 degrees for about 45 minutes. Remove from the oven. Scoop out the flesh and place in a colander lined with cheesecloth that is set over a bowl. Press down to remove any excess water. Place squash in a food processor or blender, and process until smooth.

You will have more than enough squash for this recipe. Mash and season the remaining squash for dinner, or freeze for a later use.

Squash Pie II

1 cup of cooked squash (See Squash Pie I)
2 cups of whole milk
3 common crackers, rolled and sifted
    (If you can't find common crackers, use Saltines)
⅔ cup of sugar
½ teaspoon of ground ginger
½ teaspoon of cinnamon
½ teaspoon of salt
9-inch unbaked pie crust

Preheat the oven to 425 degrees. In a small bowl, combine the sugar, spices, and salt. In a separate bowl, mix the squash, milk, and cracker crumbs together. Add the sugar mixture.

Place the unbaked pie shell on the middle rack of your oven, and slowly and carefully pour the squash mixture into the shell. Bake at 425 degrees for 15 minutes. Reduce the oven temperature to 350 degrees, and continue baking until a knife inserted in the center comes out clean, about 50 minutes.

Cool on a wire baking rack. Serve with sweetened whipped cream. Store any leftovers in the refrigerator.

Pineapple Cocoanut Pie

Coconut was spelled with an "a" in the original recipe, so I followed the tradition for the title of this recipe. Extremely yummy!

1½ cups of hot whole milk
4 tablespoons of all-purpose flour
½ teaspoon of salt
½ cup of sugar
2 extra-large egg yolks, at room temperature
1 cup of crushed pineapple, drained well
½ cup of shredded coconut (plus extra for topping)
½ teaspoon of vanilla
9-inch baked pie crust (See Note)

Preheat the oven to 350 degrees.

In the top of a double boiler over medium heat, stir together the flour, salt, and sugar. Whisk in the hot milk, stirring constantly. Cook until mixture coats the back of a wooden spoon.

In a medium bowl, beat the egg yolks until light in color. Slowly beat the hot mixture into the egg yolks, then return the mixture back into the double boiler. Cook and stir for about 3 minutes. Remove from the heat, pour into a bowl, and cover the surface with plastic wrap (this will prevent a skin from forming on the top of the filling). Set aside to cool.

Meanwhile, make a meringue using 3 extra-large egg whites (at room temperature), 6 tablespoons of superfine sugar, and ¼ teaspoon of cream of tartar. Making sure your mixing bowl and beaters are clean and grease-free, whip the egg whites until soft peaks form. Slowly add the superfine sugar and cream of tartar, and continue whipping until firm and glossy. Sugar should be completely dissolved.

Into the cooled pie filling, add the drained crushed pineapple, coconut, and vanilla. Pour into the baked pie crust. Cover with the meringue. Sprinkle with additional coconut. Bake for about 15 minutes, or until meringue and coconut are nicely browned.

Cool to room temperature. Place pie in the refrigerator, and cut when thoroughly chilled. (This will ensure that the filling sets properly;

otherwise you will have an oozy and unattractive piece of pie.)

Note: To bake a pie crust before filling (called a blind crust), fit the pie crust dough into the pie plate; cover with a piece of parchment paper and fill with either pie weights (found at kitchen supply stores) or dried beans. Bake at 350 degrees for 30 minutes; remove parchment paper and beans, and cook for 5 to 10 minutes or until lightly browned. (Covering and filling the crust with the weights or beans prevents the crust from shrinking and bubbling.)

Apple Lemon Pie

This makes a very sweet and tart pie. As with Mother Earle's Lemon Pie recipe, you may want to omit the lemon rind.

3 Cortland apples, peeled, cored, and chopped
1 cup of sugar
1 extra-large egg
Rind and juice of 1 lemon
Double crust for 9-inch pie

Preheat the oven to 350 degrees. Line a 9-inch pie plate with one crust. Spread chopped apple on top. Whisk together the sugar, egg, lemon juice, and lemon rind. Pour over the apples and top with the other crust. Brush the top crust with a little milk, and sprinkle with sugar. Make a few slits in the top, and bake for about 40 to 45 minutes. Cool completely on a wire baking rack before slicing. Serve with whipped cream.

Butter Pie

This is a custard-type pie.

2 cups of hot whole milk
¼ cup of unsalted butter, at room temperature
1 rounded ½ cup of sugar
1 tablespoon of all-purpose flour
Pinch of salt
2 beaten eggs
1 teaspoon of vanilla
9-inch unbaked pie crust

Preheat the oven to 450 degrees. In a medium saucepan, stir together the sugar, flour, and salt; cream in the butter. Over medium heat, stir in the hot milk, and cook about 5 minutes, stirring constantly. Whisk some of the hot mixture into the beaten eggs, and return to pan. Continue cooking and stirring over medium heat until the mixture coats the back of a wooden spoon.

Strain the mixture through a colander into a bowl to remove any egg solids. Stir in the vanilla. Pour into the pie crust, and bake at 450 degrees for 10 minutes. Reduce the oven temperature to 325 degrees, and cook for another 20 minutes or until set. Cool on a wire baking rack, then refrigerate and slice when thoroughly chilled.

Cream Pie

Will someone please tell me how something that is so simple to make can taste so outrageously good?

½ cup of sugar
3 heaping teaspoons of cornstarch
2 extra-large egg yolks, beaten
Pinch of salt
2 cups of hot whole milk
1 teaspoon of vanilla
9-inch baked pie crust
¼ cup of flaked or shredded coconut

Preheat the oven to 350 degrees. In the top of a double boiler over simmering water, mix the sugar and cornstarch; stir in the beaten egg yolks and salt. Slowly stir in the hot milk and cook, stirring constantly, until the mixture thickens. Remove from the heat, cool slightly, and add the vanilla.

Make a meringue (see page 94). Pour the filling into the baked pie crust, top with the meringue, and sprinkle with coconut.

Bake for about 12 to 15 minutes, or until meringue and coconut are toasty brown.

Savories

Scotch Potatoes

Scotch Potatoes

I've made this recipe with both a medium white sauce and the thick sauce that the original recipe called for. The medium sauce makes the dish creamier and less heavy. Try it both ways and see for yourself which way you prefer.

4 medium Yukon Gold potatoes, peeled and cut into ¼-inch slices
3 medium yellow onions, peeled and cut into ¼ inch slices
1 teaspoon of kosher salt
¼ teaspoon of freshly ground black pepper
1 cup of grated sharp cheddar cheese
   (I love a nice English cheddar if you can find some.)

Boil the potatoes and onions in salted water until potatoes just start to soften, about 8 minutes (test with a paring knife). Drain and place in a large bowl. Sprinkle with the salt and pepper. Toss gently, and place in a 2-quart buttered casserole dish. Cover this with a white sauce (recipe follows), and top with the cheese. Bake uncovered at 400 degrees for 25 minutes. Remove from the oven, and wait 10 minutes before delving in.

Thick White Sauce
4 tablespoons of unsalted butter
4 tablespoons of flour
Dash of salt and white pepper
1 cup of whole milk

Medium White Sauce
2 tablespoons of unsalted butter
2 tablespoons of flour
Dash of salt and white pepper
1 cup of whole milk

Melt the butter over low heat. Whisk in the flour, salt, and pepper. Cook, stirring, for 1 minute. Add the milk all at once, and whisk until thick and bubbly.

Meatloaf With Rolled Oats

This moist, simple, and flavorful meatloaf is delicious served with the Scotch Potatoes and buttered sweet peas. It is also good with homemade cranberry sauce. Make sure you use the old-fashioned rolled oats and not the quick oats, or you will end up with a gummy loaf.

1 pound of meatloaf mix or ⅓ lb. each of ground beef, veal, and pork
1 extra-large egg, beaten
½ cup of whole milk
¾ cup of old-fashioned rolled oats
1 teaspoon of poultry seasoning
½ cup of finely diced celery
½ cup of finely diced Vidalia onion
1½ teaspoons of salt
½ teaspoon of black pepper

Preheat the oven to 350 degrees. Line a small cookie sheet with aluminum foil.

In a large bowl, mix together all of the ingredients except the meat. Add the meat(s), and with freshly washed hands, mix all ingredients until well incorporated. Place on the cookie sheet, and form into an oblong shape. Bake for about 50 minutes, or until an instant-read thermometer reaches 165 degrees.

Remove from the oven, and let the meatloaf rest for 10 minutes before slicing.

If you are a gravy fan, serve slices of this old-fashioned staple with my homemade version: Melt 2 tablespoons of unsalted butter in a 2-quart saucepan over medium heat. Whisk in 2 tablespoons of flour, ¼ teaspoon of salt, and a dash of white pepper. Cook and stir about 2 minutes; then whisk in 2 cups of hot chicken stock or broth (canned is fine, but homemade is better). Reduce heat to medium-low, and continue cooking and stirring until the mixture thickens.

Salad Dressing

In the "olden days," cooked salad dressing or mayonnaise dressing was used in meat, chicken, and fish salads. The meat and poultry were highly seasoned and cooked, and bones, skin, and fat were removed when cooled. Then the meat was cut into cubes and "dressed" with the following:

1 cup of whole milk
½ tablespoon of salt
½ cup of sugar
1 tablespoon of all-purpose flour
1 tablespoon of dry mustard
¼ cup of unsalted butter
1 extra-large egg, beaten
½ cup of apple cider vinegar

Scald the milk in a small saucepan over low heat. Whisk in the salt, sugar, flour, and dry mustard. Stir in the butter until melted.

Whisk a small amount of the hot milk into the beaten egg, then whisk back into the pan. Continue cooking and stirring until the mixture becomes thick (a good 10 minutes). Remove from heat, and whisk in the apple cider vinegar. Cool slightly at room temperature, then chill thoroughly in refrigerator.

Meat Salad

This is the original recipe.

Cold meat, chopped fine, covered with mayonnaise dressing, and decorated with rings of hard-boiled eggs and parsley make a delicious supper salad when placed on nice crisp lettuce leaves.

Jazzy Ham Salad

Here is my version of an old-fashioned meat salad. Serve the same as the above recipe on a warm summer evening. Don't forget the iced tea!

1 one pound ham steak (precooked)
⅛ cup of finely chopped Vidalia onion
⅛ cup of finely chopped celery
½ cup of chopped Jazz apple, peeled and cut into ¼-inch diced pieces
4.25 ounces of apple juice (small juice box)
1 tablespoon of honey
1 tablespoon of cold unsalted butter
¼ cup of the Salad Dressing recipe

In a small saucepan over high heat, bring the apple juice and honey to a boil. Lower the heat to medium high, and reduce the liquid until it becomes slightly thickened. Remove the pan from the heat, and stir in the cold butter. Set aside while searing the ham steak.

Pat the ham steak with a dry towel to remove excess moisture. Heat a large sauté pan over medium high heat. Lightly spray the ham steak on both sides with canola cooking spray (using canola oil with not impart any additional flavors), and sear on both sides. (You should hear a very loud sizzle when you place the ham in the pan. This will sear it quickly, and keep the ham from drying out.)

Remove the ham steak to a plate, and brush both sides with the apple juice/honey reduction. Cover and cool to room temperature. Remove the bone and any fat, then chop into ¼-inch diced pieces.

Place the diced ham, onion, celery, and apple in a large bowl. Stir to combine. Add the Salad Dressing, and stir well to coat all the ingredients.

Ma, Gram, and my daughter Maria having some holiday fun

Through the years, holidays with my family brought lots of laughs, and Gram was often a major supplier of them. She would never accept an invitation to Thanksgiving or Christmas dinner unless she brought something. Her repertoire of contributions would include one or more of the following: date rolls, boiled onions, gelatin salad, or cranberry bread.

I think we all silently groaned when she brought the gelatin salads. Nobody but her and my teetotaling great aunt seemed to enjoy them. As they say, there are exceptions to every rule, and one year her salad made for some shameful fun.

When Gram came through the kitchen door carrying her wobbly side dish for a Thanksgiving feast that year, she whispered to me with a mischievous glint in her eye, "I put some wine it, but don't tell Aunt Vera." I discreetly took everyone aside before dinner and relayed this information. When dinner was ready and the table was set, we all took our seats, waited, and watched to see if the spiked side dish would somehow affect our aunt. Sure enough, about a quarter of the way through the meal, Aunt Vera's face turned rather rosy. No one dared to exchange glances for fear of bursting into laughter. All the while, Gram just sat there enjoying her feast and never revealed even a hint of her deviltry.

Sandwich Filling

This makes a wonderful dip for raw veggies. You can serve it on saltines, as suggested in the original recipe, but I found it a little too salty. It can also be used as a filling for finger sandwiches for a party along with a glass of chilled wine or an ice-cold beer.

1 5.75-ounce jar of Spanish olives, drained
8-ounces cream cheese, softened and cut into chunks
¼ of a large Vidalia onion, roughly chopped
1 hard-boiled egg, chopped
Freshly ground black pepper
8 to 10 drops of your favorite hot sauce

In the bowl of a food processor, pulse the onion until finely chopped, scrape down the sides of the bowl, and pulse again a few more times.

Add the olives and egg, and pulse about 4 times. Remove the top of the food processor, and distribute the chunks of cream cheese evenly around the bowl. Cover and pulse until all of the ingredients are well combined. Sprinkle with black pepper and hot sauce, and pulse a few more times.

Macaroni And Tuna Fish Salad Remake

1 can of tuna fish packed in olive oil, drained
¼ cup of chopped celery
¼ cup of chopped red pepper
⅛ cup of finely diced red onion
1 cup of pasta, cooked, drained, and cooled
  (I use elbows or small shells)
1 tablespoon of chopped parsley
2 tablespoons of red wine vinegar
1 teaspoon of sugar
Dash of salt and pepper
¼ teaspoon of Dijon mustard
2–3 tablespoons of extra virgin olive oil

In a medium bowl, make the dressing by whisking together the vinegar, salt, pepper, sugar, and Dijon mustard. Whisk in the olive oil until smooth.

Flake the tuna fish and remove any bones. Place the tuna and remaining ingredients (celery through parsley) in the bowl with the dressing. Toss to combine and coat.

To serve: Line a chilled plate with chopped or shredded iceberg lettuce, place a scoop of salad on top, and sprinkle with additional finely diced red pepper.

The camp at Square Pond

A real outdoors gal, Gram loved smelling the fresh ocean air and the fragrant scent of sweet fern in the woods. Before the purchase of the Happy Retreat, she and Sonny owned a camp on Square Pond in Acton, Maine. The pond was really a lake that was surrounded by acres of forested land.

Fishing Derby
Square Pond
April 25, 1948
Arline's first prize
salmon
1 lb. 7 ozs - 17 inches

Gram and her prize fish
from the Fishing Derby

During hunting season, Gram would accompany Sonny into these woodlands on his quest for deer. I asked her once if she ever shot at a deer herself.

She said, "Oh, no, I just liked being out in the woods. I used to go fishing at the pond with the men, though, but they always got mad at me because I caught the biggest fish."

At the age of 85 and nostalgic for those happy times, Gram acquired for herself a complimentary hunting and fishing license from the State of Maine.

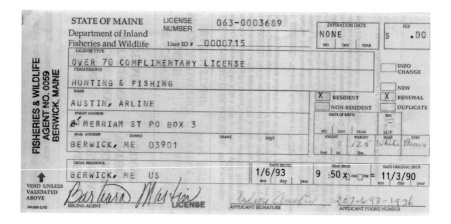

Enjoying some rest at the lake: Sonny, Bootsie, and Susie

Creamed Codfish

The codfish in this recipe could easily be replaced by some prize salmon.

2 tablespoons of all-purpose flour
2 tablespoons of unsalted butter
2 cups of whole milk
One pound or 2 cups of cooked and flaked codfish
2 chopped hard-boiled eggs
½ cup of finely diced green pepper
1 tablespoon of sharp cheddar cheese
2 extra-large eggs, well beaten
Salt and Pepper

In a 3-quart saucepan, melt the butter over medium heat. Whisk in the flour, and cook for 1 minute. Whisk in the whole milk. Cook and stir until it becomes thick. Add the cooked codfish, hard-boiled eggs, green pepper, and cheese, stirring until cheese is melted.

Take a little of this sauce and whisk it into the beaten eggs, then quickly stir back into the pan. Cook and stir until the sauce just starts to become thick again, being careful not to let it curdle. Remove from the heat and season with salt and pepper. Serve on hot buttered noodles with some fresh green beans and a crisp salad on the side.

Strawberry Shortcake

Because this was the last recipe I tested, I decided to place it here in keeping with Gram's philosophy that no meal is complete without dessert. We consumed plenty of this happy ending at her summertime retreat, although the "cake" consisted of commercially produced sponge-cake shells.

2 cups of all-purpose flour
2 teaspoons of sugar
4 teaspoons of baking powder
½ teaspoon of salt
¼ cup of cold unsalted butter
1 cup of whole milk

Preheat the oven to 425 degrees. Grease two 8-inch round cake pans with unsalted butter.

In the bowl of a food processor, pulse the flour, sugar, baking powder, and salt together a few times. Cut the butter into cubes, and scatter over the dry ingredients in the bowl. Pulse until the mixture resembles coarse crumbs. With the processor running, pour in the milk through the feed tube, and process until all ingredients are moist.

Place the dough on a LIGHTLY floured board and divide in half. Pat into the prepared pans. Bake for 12 to 15 minutes. Remove from the pans and place on a wire baking rack. Immediately spread each cake with softened *salted* butter. Place one layer on a platter (top side down) and cover with sweetened diced strawberries and a layer of vanilla whipped cream. Place the other cake layer on top (top side up) and cover with more berries, topping those with more of the vanilla whipped cream.

Vanilla Whipped Cream: Beat 1 pint of heavy cream at high speed with an electric mixer until it starts to thicken. Add 4 tablespoons of confectioners' sugar and 1 teaspoon of vanilla bean paste; continue beating until thick and luscious.

'Til we meet again!

Afterword

As this book took shape, I had an overwhelming desire to learn more about Gram's heritage. Road trips took me to the libraries of Dover, New Hampshire, Berwick and Springvale, Maine and the town of Lebanon, Maine. I visited graveyards, monuments, and churchyards where evidence of her ancestors' existence is displayed. I connected with distant Knox cousins whose brief association left me thirsty for proof of the Scottish heritage that Gram said existed. All the while, these detours gave me the impetus to keep testing recipes and writing, and kept Gram ever closer to my heart.

So far I've amassed a wealth of information to pass on to future generations, and I'm not done yet. Isn't it amazing how one simple act can precipitate such curiosity and accomplishments?

With every pinch of this and a dash of that, Gram's mystical presence guided me along. It was as if a path had been laid before me as I found the tools I needed at every turn, whether it was research materials to perfect a recipe or a photograph to highlight a story.

Call it fate, kismet, or karma, my mother was meant to find these recipes, and I was meant to tell a story. Things happen at an appointed place and time for a reason. I believe there truly are no coincidences. Even dreams can contain messages of importance if you are open-minded enough to try and analyze them.

Not long after I started working on this book, Gram appeared to me in a dream. I was in the hallway of a school, and I could feel her presence as she guided me to a row of lockers. I was to look for locker #847. When I found this locker, I opened it with a key, and discovered a black spiral-bound notebook with handwritten recipes inside. End of dream.

The next day I called my mother to tell her about this nighttime occurrence. She said, "Oh, there was a book of recipes like that that Grammie had."

I said, "Why didn't you tell me?"

Her reply: "I forgot about it." (I'll be going through *her* trash any day now.)

Anyway, it seems that my Aunt Betty (Ma's sister), who lived in Virginia at the time, had possession of it. I called my aunt, told her about my venture and the dream, and she said she would be happy to send it to me.

When I received the package in the mail from Aunt Betty, I couldn't believe it when I opened it—there inside was the exact book that Gram had led me to inside that locker. Coincidence? I think not.

Toward the end of this project, when self-doubt started to steal my enthusiasm, I threw up my hands one day and said to myself, "What am I doing? Who do I think I am trying to get a book published? Is anybody going to even like these recipes?"

That night I had another visit from Gram.

I was hiding in the bushes in front of Gram's house on Merriam Street. As I emerged from them (and out of hiding), I passed by that westward-facing front porch, and turned toward the driveway leading to the back of the house. Walking by a window, I saw Gram inside cleaning it with a newspaper and glaring at me. It was evident that she was angry. Next, I went into the garage where my mother was moving plastic bins around. She picked up a plastic wastebasket and smelled the inside. I asked her, "What does it smell like? Does it stink?"

She said, "I don't know." End of dream. (My mother had never seen this book before publication, so the symbolism of this scene seems plausible, because she wouldn't know whether it stank or not.)

I called Mom the next day, and believe it or not, Gram visited her the previous night too! My mother's dream involved one of her cousins, me, Gram, and stuffed animals. Particularly, one that Ma had given to Gram when she was in a nursing home. It was a pug dog like Gram's beloved Susie.

At the time, I was in custody of this treasured gift, and had it in a bag to give to Goodwill. (Talk about discarding sentimental family heirlooms.) I had this overwhelming feeling that Gram was none too pleased with my plans to give away her cherished present. The little stuffed dog was quickly rescued from the donation bag, and I gave it a prominent seat on the couch in my computer room.

Piece it all together and my interpretation is this: Gram wanted me to write this book, and didn't want me to give up on it—for whatever reason, and Susie the pug dog kept a watchful eye on me until the last sentence was finished.

Lisa Canino
May 2014

Acknowledgments

First and foremost, I am indebted to my mother, Marge, whose rescue made this all possible. Hope I've made you proud, Ma.

While images of my remarkable Gram kept me occupied in the kitchen and at the keyboard, voices of wisdom from those who instructed me in the classroom, culinary lab, and workplace were ever present in my mind. I will be forever grateful that you taught this middle-aged gal to believe in herself. Listed alphabetically, as you have all played an important role in the completion of this book: Larry Days, Joe Foster, George Fowler, Charles Galemmo, Chef Patrice Gerard, Patty Roche, Darlene Saltz, and Genie Zampieri. An extra thank you goes to Genie Zampieri for her friendship and help with the early editing.

Heartfelt appreciation is given to authors Steve Hrehovcik and Heather Trefethen, for sharing their knowledge of the writing and publishing world.

Nanci, Kathie, and Sue are three wonderful friends who were always willing to lend an ear, offer a helpful suggestion, and give much needed moral support. They deserve a big round of applause!!!

Lots of love goes to my daughter Andrea for her help with taste testing, and for sharing her computer knowledge. She helped me get past the daunting hurtle of tracking and editing, and I couldn't have managed it without her. She lent an ear on many occasions to my frustrated whining and always encouraged me to have patience. Bountiful thanks!!!

There have been others along this literary and culinary journey whose enthusiasm propelled me to complete my labor of love. You know who you are and I thank you.

Many thanks to the cheerful and helpful staff at Maine Authors Publishing for giving this pioneer author the opportunity to see the fruits of my labor in print. I'd like to give special thanks to Lindy Gifford for her beautiful layout and design work. She spent hours dealing with my many changes and created a top-notch finished product.

In closing, I would like to give a humongous thanks to the best daughters a mother could ask for. They have faithfully supported me in all of my endeavors and their love is always there when I need it. More than any others, Andrea and Maria, this book is for you.

Resource Materials

Better Homes and Gardens. *Better Homes and Gardens New Cookbook*. Revised Edition, Des Moines, IA: Meredith Corporation, 1976.

Bowles, Ella Shannon and Dorothy S. Towle. *Secrets of New England Cooking*. Mineola, NY: Dover Publications, 2000.

Cast Iron Collector. "Gem and Muffin Pans." *The Cast Iron Collector*. 2010–2014. 27 May 2014. www.castironcollector.com/gems.php.

Myers, Barbara. *Woman's Day Old-Fashioned Desserts*. Philadelphia and New York: CBS Consumer Publishing and J. B. Lippincott Company, 1978.

Platt, June. *June Platt's New England Cookbook*. First Ed. Canada and Kingsport, TN: McClelland and Stewart, Ltd., Kingsport Press, Inc., 1971.

Standish, Marjorie. *Cooking Down East*. Portland, ME: *Maine Sunday Telegram*, Guy Gannett Publishing Co., 1969.

Standish, Marjorie. *Keep Cooking the Maine Way*. 10th Printing, Portland, ME: *The Maine Sunday Telegram*, Guy Gannett Publishing, 1973.

Wolcott, Imogene. *The Yankee Cookbook*. New York: Coward-McCann, Inc., 1939.

Wiggins, Ruth, and Loana Shibles. *All Maine Cooking*. 12th Printing, Rockland, ME: Courier-Gazette, Inc., December, 1974.

Ziemann, Hugo, and Mrs. F. L. Gillette. *White House Cookbook*. Reprint, Bedford, MA: Applewood Books, 1 October, 2007.